Mies van der Rohe

Jean-Louis Cohen

E & FN SPON
An Imprint of Chapman & Hall

London · Glasgow · Weinheim · New York · Tokyo · Melbourne · Madras

Published by E & FN Spon, an imprint of Chapman & Hall, 2–6 Boundary Row, London SE1 8HN, UK

Chapman & Hall, 2–6 Boundary Row, London SE1 8HN, UK

Blackie Academic and Professional, Wester Cleddens Road, Bishopbriggs, Glasgow G64 2NZ, UK

Chapman & Hall GmbH, Pappelallee 3, 69469 Weinheim, Germany

Chapman & Hall USA, 115 Fifth Avenue, New York, NY 10003, USA

Chapman & Hall Japan, ITP-Japan, Kyowa Building, 3F, 2-2-1 Hirakawacho, Chiyoda-ku, Tokyo 102, Japan

Chapman & Hall Australia, 102 Dodds Street, South Melbourne, Victoria 3205, Australia

Chapman & Hall India, R. Seshadri, 32 Second Main Road, CIT East, Madras 600 035, India

English language edition 1996

© 1996 E & FN Spon

Original French language edition *Mies van der Rohe*, © 1994, Éditions Hazan.

Translated by Maggie Rosengarten

Typeset in 11/12.3pt Rockwell by Photoprint, Torquay, Devon
Printed in Hong Kong

ISBN 0 419 20330 3

A catalogue record for this book is available from the British Library

Contents

Ludwig Mies van der
Rohe, Berlin, 1934.

Mies today

The following pages may seem presumptuous. To try to convey in such a slender volume the depth and scope of the contribution of Ludwig Mies van der Rohe to the architecture of this century is no easy task, especially now that his thinking, his career, and his unbuilt designs have been illuminated by the publications, both in Europe and in the United States, which accompanied or followed the centenary of his birth.[1] Previously, apart from the occasional creative *aperçu*, the accepted image of Mies van der Rohe's work was based on a small number of buildings and a collection of aphorisms worn out by repetitive use or misuse. The 'Mies effect' relied on simplifications and short-cuts even more schematic than those which were just beginning to be discredited in the study of Le Corbusier. But if the mausoleum history has raised for the German-American architect all too often turns out to be built upon textual and visual falsifications – the paucity of source material being in no way compensated for by the accumulation of clichés and shallow half-truths – the flood of detail and anecdote released by the opening of the archives has, fortunately, been accompanied by a body of refreshing reinterpretations, which effectively compensate for decades of generalization.[2]

Since the 1930s Mies's own uncommunicative nature – he always had the greatest difficulty writing texts more than half a page long – encouraged the growth of a myth which was substantiated by first-hand witnesses such as Philip Johnson, then by historians such as Arthur Drexler and by former staff members at his Chicago office. This rendered still more deafening the silence of Sigfried Giedion, who omitted Mies from several successive editions of *Space, Time and Architecture*, that monumental chronicle of the Modern Movement.[3] It was the many holes in the fabric of knowledge that afforded such scope to sensational analyses concerning, for example, Mies's relationship with the Nazi regime;[4] more inspired interpretations appeared from the mid 1970s, and their authenticity was put to the test at the time of the centenary. The most penetrating of the sworn enemies of the Modern Movement then saw a mere representation of 'the spirit of the triumphant industrial world' in an architecture reflecting 'the expressway, fast bucks, nuclear wars'[5] – even though most research tended to reinforce the image of a Mies who profoundly respected the grand edifices of European history.

Investigation into his correspondence and designs reveals a

[1] The four publications marking the new historiographic situation concern respectively Mies's houses, philosophy, biography and design work: Wolf Tegethoff, *Mies van der Rohe; die Villen und Landhausprojekte*, Krefeld/Essen, Verlag Richard Bacht GmbH, 1981 (in English: Cambridge (Mass.), London, MIT Press, 1985); Fritz Neumeyer, *Mies van der Rohe, das Kunstlose Wort: Gedanken zur Baukunst*, Berlin, Siedler Verlag, 1986 (in English: Cambridge (Mass.), London, MIT Press, 1991); Franz Schulze, *Mies van der Rohe: a Critical Biography*, Chicago, University of Chicago Press, 1985; Arthur Drexler (editor), *The Mies van der Rohe Archive*, New York, Garland, 1986–93.

[2] The Mies van der Rohe Archive essentially comprises two collections: the general practice correspondence, lodged in the Library of Congress (LC) – approximately 22 000 documents; and the drawings, correspondence and manuscripts relating to the plans, lodged in The Museum of Modern Art (MoMA) – approximately 20 000 items – to which are added the collections of the Bauhaus-Archiv of Berlin and other institutions.

[3] It was only in the last issues of *Space, Time and Architecture* that Mies really appeared; on this subject, see: Fritz Neumeyer, 'Giedion en Mies van der Rohe: een paradox in de historiografie van het Moderne', *Archis*, April 1992, pp. 47–51.

[4] Elaine S. Hochman, *Architects of Fortune: Mies van der Rohe and the Third Reich*, New York, Weidenfeld and Nicholson, 1989. An infinitely more solid and qualified view of the relations between Mies and German politics is given by Richard Pommer; see: 'Mies van der Rohe and the Political Ideology of the Modern Movement in Architecture', in Franz Schulz (editor), *Mies van der Rohe: Critical Essays*, New York, MoMA, Cambridge (Mass.), MIT Press, 1990, pp. 96–145.

[5] Maurice Culot and Léon Krier, 'A European Perspective on the Mies van der Rohe Centennial', in *The Chicago Architecture Annual*, Chicago, Metropolitan Press Publications, 1986, pp. 13–14.

[6] On the new generation of publications, see: Juan Pablo Bonta, 'The Analysis of Mies: A New Language or Old Clichés?', *Design Book Review*, No. 10, autumn 1986, pp. 20–29, and 'Mies as Text', *Design Book Review*, No. 13, autumn 1987, pp. 20–25; Winfried Nerdinger, 'Nachlese zum 100. Geburtstag; neue Literatur zu Mies van der Rohe', *Kunstchronik*, vol 41, No. 8, August 1988, pp. 419–29.

[7] Philip Johnson, in John W. Cook, Heinrich Klotz, *Conversations with Architects*, New York, Praeger, 1973, p. 73.

[8] Elaine S. Hochman, *Architects of Fortune: Mies van der Rohe and the Third Reich*, op. cit., p. 24.

[9] Francesco Dal Co has reproduced and explained these notes: 'Il centenario di Mies', *Domus*, No. 668, January 1986, pp. 8–11.

new picture of the architect, with his intellectual, philosophical and religious outlook more clearly defined.[6] It is this view of Mies as seen through his daily work, his professional strategies and his philosophical reflections, which makes possible such an undertaking as the present book. Whereas his architecture was once perceived as just a closed set of icons, he now appears a more cultivated figure than for example Philip Johnson was prepared to admit when he sarcastically alluded to the three thousand books which Mies said he had in Germany.[7] Mies's desire to be considered as a profound thinker, and his propensity for aphorisms and sententious statements, have been unfairly interpreted as indicative of 'intellectual insecurity',[8] but now that his philosophical and literary contacts and interests are better known, the picture becomes more complex.

The same is true for his architectural work, built and unbuilt, designed over six decades of professional activity. In discussion this body of work is often reduced to clichés about the 'open plan' or 'modern space' or an obsession with structural engineering; actually it is the product of a philosophy of construction and the definition of new spaces, which is inseparable from a concern for order, both structural and monumental. A solitary figure, whose work was rooted in the technology and ethos of the second machine age, Mies was no nihilist. The direction of his work cannot be explained simply by his own experiences; it is inseparable from explicit and implicit relationships established with several generations of architects – as is shown by the notes written in 1959 for his acceptance speech for the RIBA gold medal, in which he lists the inspirations in his initial quest for an understanding of architecture: Messel, Behrens, Olbrich, Berlage, Lutyens, Voysey, Baillie-Scott and Mackintosh.[9] Indeed, beyond the figures of his elders, Berlage and Behrens, Mies never lost sight of either Viollet-le-Duc (with his precept that 'any form which is not determined by the structure must be rejected'), or Schinkel, whom he considered 'the greatest classicist we had.'[10]

Further back in history Mies always maintained an intellectual affinity with medieval architecture and with Greece, a world (unlike Rome) of *culture* and not of mere *civilization*.[11] For the same reasons as Auguste Perret, he offered a new interpretation of the ideal of a 'Graeco-Gothic' architecture, as expressed by the French rationalists in the nineteenth century. Unlike Perret, he did this by integrating the issues of modern art into his work. His relationships with his contemporaries remained more complex:

Mies never missed an opportunity to point out everything that separated him from individuals like Walter Gropius, Frank Lloyd Wright and Le Corbusier and from avant-garde groups such as De Stijl and the Constructivists.[12] Presenting himself, in the interviews that he gave at the end of his life, as a solitary hero who rebelled against passing fashions, and reproaching his contemporaries for their obsession with the present and neglect of the past, Mies emphasized the distinction between a healthy sense of continuity and mere historicism, by conscientiously applying the slogan formulated in his manifesto of 1924, *Baukunst und Zeitwille!* (Construction and Contemporaneity!), which states that 'It is not possible to go forward while looking back'.[13] A year later, he confirmed his strong desire to free *Bauerei* – 'buildery', we might say, as distinct from architecture – from aesthetic fancy, to give the word *Bauen*, 'to build', its full force.[14] Drawn one way towards constructive rationality, and the other way towards the search for a *firmitas* or solidity that would be more institutional than physical, Mies always saw architecture as the union of two inseparables: the expression of the 'will of the age' (*Zeitwille*), and that of those unchanging values that require to be interpreted in a Platonic perspective.[15] The monoliths of steel and glass that he built in American cities reflect this inclination towards *Bauen*: building using a limited repertoire of forms devoid of aesthetic intention and intended to *serve* rather than to interpret.

Mies van der Rohe's belief in Order and Truth, independent of human circumstances, evolved over many years, and found its most obvious expression in his personal relationships with his clients and with those closest to him. There has been much – sometimes too much – talk of his lack of interest in some clients' expectations. It has been suggested, although unfairly, that the Farnsworth house is totally uninhabitable;[16] it is true that the Esters sweltered behind the glass of their fully south-facing house, and the residents of 860 Lake Shore Drive had no cooling system. Trivial by comparison with the daily tribulations of the inhabitants of houses built by Le Corbusier or Frank Lloyd Wright, these clients' troubles were accepted with a certain amused condescension by Mies. In 1930 he imposed on the Tugendhats, in their Brno villa, a whole set of furniture which they 'must learn to love'; in 1959 he declared that 'we should treat our clients as children, not as architects'.[17]

Here we see his character. Distant with his family, hostile to all emotions – 'everybody has them, and that's the hell of our age' –

[10] 'Ludwig Mies van der Rohe', *Architectural Association Journal*, vol. 75, No. 834 (July-August 1959, p. 29 (talks held by Mies on 27 May 1959 at the Architectural Association).

[11] Mies van der Rohe, interview with Peter Carter, *20th Century*, spring 1964, p. 139.

[12] Mies van der Rohe, interview with Peter Blake, in *Four Great Makers of Modern Architecture*, New York, Columbia University, typed, pp. 93–104 (transcription of symposium held from March to May 1961).

[13] Mies van der Rohe, 'Baukunst und Zeitwille!', *Der Querschnitt*, No. 4, 1924, p. 31 and following.

[14] Mies van der Rohe, 'Bauen', *G*, No. 2, September 1923, p. 1.

[15] Massimo Cacciari, 'Mies's Classics', *Res.* No. 16, autumn 1988, pp. 9–16.

[16] This is particularly the view of Elaine S. Hochman in *Architects of Fortune: Mies van der Rohe and the Third Reich*, op. cit., pp. 56–7.

[17] 'Ludwig Mies van der Rohe', *Architectural Association Journal*, loc. cit.

[18] Mies van der Rohe, '6 Students Talk with Mies', in *Student Publications of the School of Design*, Raleigh, vol. 2, No. 3, spring 1952, p. 25.

he had, by his own admission, 'nothing of the sentimentalist' about him.[18] Late in life, a monolithic figure clad in wool and silk, his arthritis rendered him still more an immovable object; and this elegant massiveness in some way served as a human metaphor for his American architecture.

What, then, can be the role of this book in the face of Mies's monumental achievement? It is no longer possible to restrict a commentary to the finished work of his 'major' buildings alone, as in the compact monographs published from the 1960s onward; but at the same time the limitations of this series make it impossible to cover all the ramifications of ten years' research. I have therefore decided to concentrate on a limited number of designs and structures, which are discussed in depth, with full reference to their specific historical and biographical significance. In particular, I have tried to let Mies speak for himself: something he did more often than people might like to think. His own comments on his work, often retrospective, will in this way give a personal resonance to the places that he created – a resonance that he would no doubt not have wanted, but without which they are difficult to understand.

First endeavours in Berlin (1908–14)

Ludwig Mies built his first house in Neubabelsberg at the age of twenty. Like the chalets built by the young Charles-Édouard Jeanneret at La Chaux-de-Fonds – which he meticulously deleted from his *Oeuvre complète* in spite of the favourable publicity they attracted from the time they were built – Mies's early creations remained absent from his major exhibitions and from publications on his work until the 1980s. And yet his early career led him in just a few years from a provincial childhood and adolescence in the Rhineland to Berlin, where he became an undoubted fashionable success.

The impression left by his early life in Aachen remained strong. He often claimed that his Catholic family had 'Celtic' origins. He was one of five children born to Michael Mies and Amalie Rohe.[19] Michael Mies was a builder and stonemason, and Ludwig was steeped in the building trade from the outset. The pejorative connotations of his father's surname[20] led Ludwig to coin another one, incorporating his mother's maiden name, Rohe: he became Mies van der Rohe in 1921.

In a town transformed by growth and modernization, Michael Mies built fireplaces, then was employed maintaining the cathedral masonry, and built many tombs in partnership with his brother. The young Ludwig would remember the traditional houses which were progressively replaced by speculative apartment blocks, and the impression of the strength of the cathedral and the Romanesque Palatine Chapel:

> I remember seeing many old buildings in my hometown when I was young. Few of them were important buildings. They were mostly very simple, but very clear. I was impressed by the strength of these buildings because they did not belong to any epoch. They had been there for over a thousand years and were still impressive, and nothing could change that. All the great styles passed, but they were still there. They didn't lose anything and they were still as good as on the day they were built. They were medieval buildings, not with any special character but they were really *built*.[21]

Mies attended the Catholic Cathedral School from 1896 to 1899, then the Craft Day School from 1899 to 1901. Thus provided with a technical and vocational education which was not classical like that of the *Gymnasium* (which he attended for two years), he

[19] Born 27 March 1886, Maria Ludwig Michael was the youngest son. All his life he retained close ties with his eldest brother Ewald, born in 1877. Michael Mies was born in Aix on 29 March 1851, and died there on 31 December 1927; Amalie Rohe was born in Monschau on 14 April 1843, and died in Aix on 31 May 1928. Both of them were of very old Catholic descent: note concerning the Aryan credentials of the Mies family, Berlin police headquarters, 28 November 1938, MoMA, personal documents, file 1.

[20] The adjective *mies* can be translated in English as 'wretched' or 'daft'. . .

A RHINELAND CHILDHOOD

[21] Mies van der Rohe, remarks collected by Peter Carter in 'Mies van der Rohe. An Appreciation on the Occasion, this Month of his 75th Birthday', *Architectural Design*, vol 31, No. 3, March 1961, p. 97.

Bruno Paul, Westend
house, Berlin, 1906.

Bruno Paul, tennis club,
Grünewald, 1908.

completed his education with evening classes in building, civil
engineering, mathematics and life drawing.[22] Often enlisted by
his father to carve inscriptions on headstones, he worked for a
year, unpaid, as an apprentice bricklayer on local building sites.
Reminiscing in later life about his observations of brickwork, he
would stress the difficulties involved in making angles and cop-
ings, but he insisted on the value of the experience in teaching
him construction detailing.[23] Then he gained practical experience
both with craftsmen and in several architects' offices. He was
apprenticed to Max Fischer, a maker of plaster mouldings, where
he used vertical drawing boards, a habit he retained for a long
time. He then became a draughtsman, a highly valued specialist
in decorative ornament, working for the architects F. Goebbels
and (later) Albert Schneider.[24]

While working in Schneider's office on the building of the Tietz
department store, he found a copy of the literary review *Die
Zukunft*, edited by Maximilian Harden, of which he read more on
his visits to the municipal library.[25] Now that his interest had been
attracted by the intellectual life of the capital, he was persuaded
by Dulow, one of the architects in the practice, to apply for
vacancies in Berlin advertised in *Die Bauwelt*. And so he left his
native city in 1905 to start work as a draughtsman for the municipal
architect's department of the urban district of Rixdorf, to the southwest of Berlin, where under Reinhold Kiehl he designed the
panelling of the council chamber of the Town Hall – not without
some difficulty, because up until then he had only worked with
masonry.[26]

His time in the Kaiser's army was extremely short. He was
discharged after an attack of bronchitis following a collective
punishment of his unit. Back in civilian life, he came across the
architect Bruno Paul at the beginning of 1906, at the time when
the latter was moving his practice from Munich to Berlin. It was
a decisive meeting. Mies became at once a draughtsman in the
Paul office and a pupil at the two establishments where Paul
taught, enrolling in the school of the Museum of Arts and Crafts
(Kunstgewerbemuseum) and at the Institute of Fine Arts (Hochschule für bildende Künste) from the summer term of 1906 to the
summer term of 1908.[27] He had a special position in the practice,
on account of his previous practical experience of building. He
specialized in the design of furniture. Paul had long been a
successful caricaturist in the satirical magazine *Simplicissimus*;

[22] Certificate of 18 January
1956, Aix-la-Chapelle,
MoMA, personal
documents, file 3.

[23] Mies van der Rohe,
interview with Dirk Lohan,
Chicago, summer 1968 (in
German, typed), New York,
MoMA, p. 11.

[24] Proof kept in the Mies
Archive, LC, box 62.

[25] Of Nietzschian
inspiration, *Die Zukunft*
published, between 1892
and 1922, texts concerning
the architecture of Kurt
Scheffler, Henry van de
Velde and August Endell,
but also articles by the
sociologists Werner
Sombart and Georg Simmel
and the writers Heinrich
Mann and August
Strindberg.

[26] Franz Schulze, *Mies van
der Rohe: Critical Essays*,
op. cit., pp. 17–19.

[27] Hochschule für bildende
Künste, certificate of 7
February 1906, LC, box 62.

Aloïs Riehl house,
Neubabelsberg, 1907,
floor plans.

over the next few years he expanded his activity in Berlin
building blocks of flats and town houses and even fitting out the
interiors of a number of German transatlantic liners.[28]

In 1906 Joseph Popp, an assistant of the artist Emil Orlik, in whose
studio Mies was studying engraving, recommended him to the
wife of Aloïs Riehl, a professor of philosophy at Berlin University.
The Riehls were looking for a young architect to build them a
house. From them, Mies obtained his first commission at the age
of twenty, which he insisted on carrying out unaided, refusing all
offers of advice from Bruno Paul.[29] The site was in an area of
detached houses on a wooded slope behind a lake (the Griebnitzsee), in Neubabelsberg, an urban district later annexed by
Potsdam, in which Mies was to design many other houses (only
two of which, the Urbig and Mosler houses, were actually built).
Klösterli was built in 1907, a house of rendered brick, with a steep
roof. The end wall which overlooks the lake opens into a loggia,
which reproduces the rhythms used by Bruno Paul in his Westend
house, built at the same time, and is also reminiscent of Paul's
Berlin tennis club. Paul would have liked Mies to work on his
project with him.[30]

BRUNO PAUL
AND THE RIEHL
HOUSE

The house has a rectangular plan, which centres on a large hall,
opening on to two lateral alcoves and on to the loggia. The
appearance of the end wall and that of the loggia perched on a
long retaining parapet wall also recall the crematorium built by
Peter Behrens in Hagen in 1906. A degree of English influence,
received by way of Hermann Muthesius,[31] appears in the design
of the hall, whose panelling has a finesse that characterizes all of
the detailing of this remarkably compact interior right down to the
alcoves on the first floor. The kitchen, the bookcases and the
radiator grilles reflect Mies's interest in built-in furniture. The
planning of the house is dominated by the right angle between
the axis of entry and the downhill view, its lateral extension being
treated as a platform behind the retaining wall, overlooked by a
façade that seems rather compressed by the top-heavy bulk of
the roof. The detail is faithful to the Prussian tradition of the early
nineteenth century, which Paul Mebes praised in his influential
book *Um 1800*.[32]

This building, which is a remarkably mature creation for a 21
year old architect, was favourably received in the architectural
press, which stressed the 'skill' shown by an 'irreproachable'

[28] On Bruno Paul, see:
Joseph Popp, *Bruno Paul*,
Munich, F. Bruckmann,
1916; A. Ziffer (editor),
*Bruno Paul, Deutsche
Raumkunst und Architektur
zwischen Jugendstil und
Moderne*, Munich, 1992.

[29] Mies van der Rohe,
interview with Dirk Lohan,
op. cit., pp. 26–7.

[30] Fritz Neumeyer, *Mies
van der Rohe, das
Kunstlose Wort: Gedanken
zur Baukunst*, op. cit., p. 76.

[31] The impact of English
models in this house is in
my opinion overestimated
by Schink: Arnold Schink,
*Mies van der Rohe:
Beiträge zur ästhetischen
Entwicklung der
Wohnarchitektur*, Stuttgart,
Karl Krämer, 1990, p. 42.

[32] Paul Mebes, *Um 1800,
Architektur und Handwerk
im letzten Jahrhundert ihrer
Entwicklung*, Munich, F.
Bruckmann, 1908.

Aloïs Riehl house,
Neubabelsberg, 1907.
1. Overall view.
2. The entrance hall.
3. Upper floor alcove.
4. The gable over the
   valley (photo 1992).
5. The entrance (photo
   1992).

	1
4	2
5	3

Peter Behrens, *Kleinmotorenfabrik* for the AEG, Berlin-Wedding, 1910–13.

Peter Behrens, *Turbinenhalle* for the AEG, Berlin-Moabit, 1909.

work, which gave a lesson in 'balance' to Mies's older colleagues.[33]

Delighted with Mies's talents and with his company, Aloïs and Sophie Riehl included him in their social circle, in which he met some of the founders of modern Germany including the industrialist Walther Rathenau, the philosopher Werner Jaeger and the art historian Heinrich Wölfflin. Mies developed with growing freedom in this world where he met the clients of future houses, the Gerickes, Noldes, Dexels, Wolfs and Eliats. He was introduced to the ideas of Nietzsche, of which Riehl was a well known exponent.[34] His frequent visits to the Riehl household also threw him into the arms of Ada Bruhn, who, having broken off her engagement with Wölfflin, was a pupil at the Émile-Jacques Dalcroze dance school in Hellerau. Meanwhile, in 1908, the Riehls gave him a bursary which enabled him to take a six-week trip to Munich, Rome, Florence and Vicenza, with Joseph Popp. Mies was especially struck by the Palazzo Pitti and the villas of Palladio – 'not only La Rotonda, which is very formal, but also the others which are more free', he was to say sixty years later. On his return from Italy, however, he noticed the extent to which the details of the houses of Alfred Messel in Wannsee, which he discovered while he was in Risdorf, were 'more delicate than those of Palladio'. . . Mies also remembered the admiration he felt for the 'wonderful' Wertheim department store by Messel and its glass façade overlooking Potsdamer Platz.[35] Riehl's death in 1924 brought an end to a close relationship which Mies commemorated by designing the philosopher's gravestone in the Neubabelsberg cemetery.

[33] Anton Jaumann, 'Vom künstlerischen Nachwuchs, Haus Riehl', *Innendekoration*, vol. 21, July 1910, pp. 266–73, and 'Architect L. Mies, Villa des Prof. Dr. Riehl in Neubabelsberg', *Moderne Bauformen*, vol. 9, 1910, pp. 42–48.

[34] Fritz Neumeyer, *Mies van der Rohe, das Kunstlose Wort: Gedanken zur Baukunst*, op. cit., pp. 89–90.

[35] Mies van der Rohe, interview with Dirk Lohan, op. cit., p. 29.

Impressed by the qualities of the Riehl house, Paul Thiersch, manager of the Bruno Paul office, advised him to introduce himself to Peter Behrens, who took him on in October 1908. Behrens had been appointed the previous year by Emil Rathenau's AEG *Konzern* to create a corporate identity programme for its buildings, products and advertising. He had made his name in 1901 by building his own house in the artists' colony in Darmstadt, and later by his teaching and his architectural work over the following years in Düsseldorf.[36]

Mies was to declare, on one of his last trips to Berlin, that he himself had designed the courtyard elevations of Behrens's AEG-*Turbinenhalle*, which were simply defined by the plate-glass wall, the profile of the metal piers in a double T-shape and the

PETER BEHRENS AND THE ARCHITECTURE OF INDUSTRY

[36] Fritz Hoeber, *Peter Behrens*, Munich, Georg Muller & Eugen Rentsch, 1913; Stanford O. Anderson, *Peter Behrens and the New Architecture of Germany, 1900–1917*, New York, Columbia University 1968 (PhD thesis).

Peter Behrens, German Embassy, St. Petersburg, 1912 (photo 1989).

Peter Behrens, the Wiegand house, Berlin-Dahlem, 1912: entrance (photo 1990) and detail of the cornice (photo 1990).

37 Mechthild Heuser, 'Die Fenster zum Hof, Die Turbinenhalle, Behrens und Mies van der Rohe', in Hans-Georg Pfeifer (editor), Peter Behrens: 'Wer aber will sagen, was Schönheit sei?': Grafik Produktgestaltung, Architektur, Düsseldorf, Beton-Verlag, 1990, pp. 108–21.

38 Tilmann Buddensieg and Hennig Rogge, Industriekultur, Peter Behrens und die AEG, 1907–1914, Berlin, Gebr. Mann, 1979.

39 Mies van der Rohe, interview with Dirk Lohan, op. cit., p. 27.

40 On the 'sources' of Mies's architecture, see amongst others: Sandra Honey, 'Who and What Inspired Mies van der Rohe in Germany', Architectural Design, vol. 49, No. 3–4, 1979, pp. 99–102.

41 Paul Westheim, 'Mies van der Rohe, Entwicklung eines Architekten', Der Kunstblatt, No. 2, February 1927, pp. 55–62.

42 The Orianda designs would moreover haunt Mies for a long time: Wolf Tegethoff, 'Orianda-Berlin, Das Vorbild Schinkels im Werk Mies van der Rohes', Zeitschrift des Deutschen vereins für Kunst Wissenschaft, vol. 25, No. 1–4, 1985, pp. 174–84.

brick base; 'Behrens didn't realize what he was doing', said Mies: intending to build a factory, he had 'resolved all the problems of architecture'.[37] As well as this contribution, which foreshadowed the buildings of the Illinois Institute of Technology, Mies collaborated on the small motor factory (Kleinmotorenfabrik) in Wedding, Berlin.[38] For Mies and other young architects in the practice – including Walter Gropius, his future partner Adolf Meyer and Charles-Édouard Jeanneret, whom Mies remembered having 'met in a doorway'[39] – Behrens was the archetype of the Nietzschian artist who had sealed an alliance with modern industry; but he was also responsible for Mies's lifelong passion for the architecture of Karl Friedrich Schinkel.[40]

Behrens took his colleagues to look at some of Schinkel's buildings near the office in Neubabelsberg, including the mansion and garden buildings in Glienicke park and the gardener's house and the Roman baths of Charlottenhof, in Potsdam. Mies's interest in Schinkel – recorded in 1927 by Paul Westheim, who spoke of the 'amazing feeling' the two architects had in common for 'the mass, the relationships, the rhythms and the harmony of forms' – sprang from these visits.[41]

Mies wasted no time in turning his interest into practice. In 1910 he entered a competition for a monument in Bingen intended for the centenary celebrations of the birth of Bismarck which were planned for 1915. Mies visualized a stone bastion, built against the hillside overlooking the Rhine, on which a colonnade framed a rectangular space before a statue of the Iron Chancellor by his brother Ewald. There are striking affinities between the situation of this collonade and that of the palace designed by Schinkel for the Tsar at Orianda, in the Crimea.[42] On the other hand Mies felt no nostalgia for the graphic techniques of the nineteenth century and used in his submission a large collage of a photograph of the model on a photograph of the site, thus pioneering the architectural use of montage, a technique that he was to use on many subsequent occasions. Entitled 'Germany's Gratitude', his entry was on the shortlist of 40 selected out of 380 for a more detailed study, but the evident cost of its foundations meant that it was set aside.[43]

The love of Schinkel brought Mies his second commission, from the wealthy lawyer Hugo Perls, a collector of contemporary art and a fellow-enthusiast for the work of the great Prussian architect. In 1910 Perls engaged Mies, whom he had met at one of the

Hugo Perls house,
Berlin Zehlendorf, 1911:
detail of the cornice
(photo 1990), ground
floor plans and façade
overlooking the garden
(photo 1990).

artistic soirées which he organized, to build him a house at
Zehlendorf. The Perls house is a compact, stuccoed brick building. The relationship between its main block house and the roof
is very different from that in the Riehl house. The ground floor,
intended for Perls's collections, centres on a dining room
intended to contain frescoes by Max Pechstein, a *Die Brücke*
painter. It opens onto a loggia fronted by two columns, like that
of Schinkel's pavilion at Charlottenburg, but brought down to
ground level. On one side of the dining room is a study and on
the other a library and music room, with the bedrooms on the first
floor.

The Perls house reflects not only the rapport which Mies had
forged with Schinkel but also the reinterpretation of Schinkel's
work attempted by Behrens in the big house which he built at
Dahlem in the same year for Theodor Wiegand, the archaeologist
and director of the Imperial Museums in Berlin.[45] Schinkel's spirit
was transposed into the system of colonnades, into the relationship to the site with its platforms and foundations, and into the
design of the cornices of the main building, built in grey lime-
stone. Mies does not seem to have worked on this project; his
main activity with Behrens was at that time the supervision of the
building of the German embassy in Saint Petersburg.[46] He
worked on site on this project in 1911–12, but later admitted that
he had only designed one door handle for a building for which
he seems to have cared little.[47]

> That was really a kind of palace, architecturally –
> Palladio or that sort of thing. But Behrens decided to use
> Finnish granite. That of course made all classicist details
> disappear. The character all the same was something like
> the Brandenburger Tor, something which conveys
> Berlin, and that suited Petersburg quite well . . . So under
> Behrens, I learnt grand form, if you see what I mean.[48]

In fact, Mies appears to have had some difficulty working in
Behrens's office, where, until Gropius's departure in 1910, he
found himself working under the tutelage of an architect senior to
himself and who also came from a privileged social class. He
stayed on the fringe of the activities of the Deutscher Werkbund,
in which Gropius and Behrens were involved. It was with the

[43] Max Schmidt, *Das
Bismarck Nationaldenkmal
auf der Elisenhöhe bei
Bingerbrück (Hundert
Entwürfe aus dem
Wettbewerb)*, Düsseldorf
1911.

[44] Dietrich von Beulwitz,
'The Perls' House by Mies
van der Rohe',
Architectural Design, vol.
53, No. 10–11, 1983,
pp. 63–71.

[45] Wolfram Hoepfner and
Fritz Neumeyer, *Das Haus
Wiegand von Peter
Behrens in Berlin-Dahlem:
Baugeschichte und
Kunstgegenstände eines
herrschaftlichen
Wohnhauses*, Mayence,
von Zabern, 1979.

[46] K. Schaefer, 'Gebäude
der Kaiserlich Deutschen
Botschaft in St Petersburg',
Der Profanbau, No. 12,
1914, pp. 309–24.

[47] On the experiences of
Mies in St. Petersberg, see:
Sergius Ruegenberg, 'Der
Skelettbau ist keine
Teigware', *Bauwelt*, vol. 77,
No. 11, 14 March 1986,
p. 346.

[48] 'Mies Speaks', *The
Architectural Review*, vol.
144, No. 362, December
1968, p. 451 (transcript of an
interview given to the
Berlin RIAS).

1. Competition project for a monument to Bismarck, Elisenhöhe, Bingen, 1910, side elevation (signed drawing, the Mies van der Rohe Archives, The Museum of Modern Art, New York).

2. Karl-Friedrich Schinkel, project for a palace on the Acropolis for King Othon of Greece, Athens, 1834, elevations.

3. Karl-Friedrich Schinkel, project for a summer palace at Orianda, Crimea, 1838, perspective.

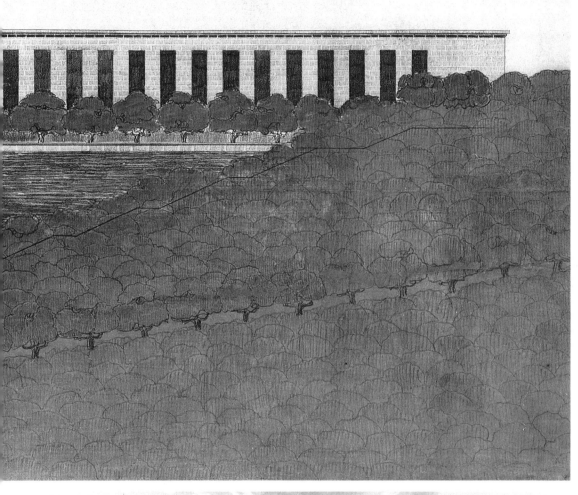

19

Project for the Anthony George Kröller and Hélène Müller house, Wassenaar, La Haye, 1912. Full size model and presentation model.

THE KRÖLLER-MÜLLER PROJECT: MIES SETS UP IN PRACTICE

commission for the Krüller-Müller house that the break came in 1912. In the spring of 1911 Behrens had received the commission for a residence which this factory-owning couple wanted to build on a piece of land near Otterlo, in the Netherlands, to house their collections of Van Gogh and other modern artists. Mies was deputed to work on Behrens's design, which was rejected after a full-size canvas mock-up had been erected on site in January 1912. The commission was then given directly to Mies. This alienated Behrens even more firmly than did Mies's growing veneration for Berlage, whom he ceaselessly praised for his 'honesty', to the profound irritation of his employer:

> Berlage's Exchange (at Amsterdam) had impressed me enormously. Behrens was of the opinion that it was all passé, but I said to him: 'Well, if you aren't badly mistaken.' He was furious; he looked as if he wanted to hit me. What interested me most in Berlage was his careful construction, honest to the bones. And his spiritual attitude had nothing to do with classicism, nothing with historic styles altogether. After Berlage I had to fight with myself to get away from the classicism of Schinkel.[49]

Taking over the Kröller-Müller project himself, Mies transformed the original design. He enlarged the building, opened it out and articulated its freely symmetrical rectilinear blocks by means of a colonnade. The linearity and the planar quality of this design explain why it was the only early work judged worthy of being

[49] 'Mies Speaks', op. cit.

20

shown in the Mies retrospective at The Museum of Modern Art in New York in 1947. Mrs Kröller's advisors, who seem to have had a penchant for Mies, nevertheless persuaded her to place him in competition with Berlage. In spite of the support given to Mies's design by the critic Julius Meier-Graefe, Mrs Krüller was persuaded by her advisor, Hendrik Peter Bremmer, who contrasted the 'art' of Berlage with Mies's supposed lack of it. Another full-size mock-up was made, and Mies was eliminated.[50]

After his Dutch experience Mies set up in independent practice: he opened an office in Steglitz, Berlin, in 1913, and married Ada Bruhn on 10 April of the same year. He lost no time in becoming absorbed in a series of plans for Berlin housing and was equally conscientious in evading the responsibilities of marital life. In 1912–13, on a plot adjacent to the Perls house in Zehlendorf, he built a residence for the engineer Ernst Werner. Its exterior design is very conservative. On a rectangular plan, with a traditional roof, the house is symmetrical in layout; only the portico on the garden front is a reminder of the Schinkelesque sympathies of its architect, who lavished great care on the design of the furniture.

In Neubabelsberg in 1913–14, Mies built a villa with solemn and chilly interiors for the banker Franz Urbig and his wife, friends and neighbours of the Riehls. Built at water level beside the Griebnitzsee, its large mass of traditional construction in rendered masonry occupies a rectangular ground plan, extended by a lakeside dining room. Mies's original design incorporated a virtually flat roof in the style of Schinkel, but Urbig objected and they agreed on the popular villa style.[51]

Although a good ten years later than the Urbig house, the villa built for the banker Georg Mosler nearby in 1924 is closely comparable. Its masses are similar, and it occupies a lakeside site below the Riehl house, with a massive loggia overlooking the lake, and a rectilinear lateral extension containing the kitchen. The plain surface of the brickwork is relieved by vertical windows with grey stone dressings; the thick mass of the walls conveys an impression of bourgeois stability.[52] After the First World War Mies was to construct three houses in Berlin with themes which were identical in their composition and their construction: the Kempner house in Charlottenburg, the Feldmann house in Grunewald and the Eichstaedt house in Zehlendorf.

Ernst Werner house, Berlin-Zehlendorf, 1912–13, façade overlooking the garden, dining room, radiator cover (photos 1990).

[50] Julius Meier-Graefe, letter to Mies, Paris, 18 November 1912, MoMA, early plans, file 1; Franz Schulze, *Mies van der Rohe Critical Essays*, op. cit., pp. 58–64.

[51] This would enable the critic Werner Hegemann to use this house in his polemics against the roof-terrace, when Mies became more radical: Werner Hegemann, 'Schräges oder flaches Dach', *Wasmuths Monatshefte für Baukunst*, May 1927, pp. 120–27.

[52] This austerity aroused the criticism of the local administration; see: Renate Petras, 'Drei Arbeiten Mies van der Rohes in Potsdam-Babelsberg', *Architektur der DDR*, vol. 23, No. 2, 1974, p. 120 and following.

Franz Urbig house, Neubabelsberg, 1917, view from the riverbank.

These buildings, which were in many respects more conservative than the Perls house seem out of keeping with the direction Mies's work was taking. In 1914 he designed a house for his own family, to be built on a plot of land which he and his wife had bought at Werder, to the west of Potsdam. Schinkelesque in its relationship to the site, defined by platforms, this design with its two sharp-edged blocks and its flat roofs points to a radically different way of thinking. In fact it was the forerunner of the new generation of projects which Mies was to design after the war.

He was not conscripted for the war until 1915, when he was stationed near Frankfurt-am-Main. After returning to Berlin for a time, he was posted in 1917 to Romania, where he spent the rest of the war. The war was largely a period of inactivity, during which he assiduously sought out the company of the sculptor Wilhelm Lehmbruck. The lessons of his early years had yet to bear fruit: through his experiences with Behrens, he had learned the importance of the connection with industry and the wealth of scope for innovation that is represented by the modern metropolis. But his successes in the world of collectors and patrons also suggested to him, and to a certain extent even to his public, the possibility of a career activity orientated towards the world of the arts.

Theoretical projects for the Metropolis (1918–24)

In 1927, when Paul Westheim published a first comprehensive view of Mies's work with the subtitle 'development of an architect', he deliberately excluded most of the pre-1914 projects, with the exception of the Kröller-Müller project and the design for the house at Werder, in which he recognized the stamp of Schinkel, and whose continuity with Mies's post-war work he stressed.[53] Such a suggestion no doubt surprised contemporary readers, because a quartet of unbuilt designs from the immediate post-war period seemed to mark an absolute break with the past. The Glass Skyscraper (in its two successive versions), the Concrete Office Building and the Concrete Country Houses certainly showed a very different profile. This new cycle began in 1921, three years after the Republican Revolution of November 1918, to which Mies seems to have been indifferent. Moreover, his initial relations with the utopian groups emerging in a Germany fizzing with new ideas were difficult, since the Kröller-Müller project, which he was later to designate as the turning point of his career, was condemned by Gropius, who in 1919 organized the exhibition in Berlin of 'Unknown architects' under the auspices of the Arbeitsrat für Kunst. There is no doubt that this led to a certain bitterness on Mies's part towards his former colleague from the Behrens office.[54]

The contribution of Mies – henceforth with the aristocratic-sounding suffix 'van der Rohe' – to the competition for the Friedrichstrasse skyscraper, submitted at the end of January 1922, confirmed his originality. The notion of the skyscraper had been posed before the war in the debate on the future of the centre of Berlin, in particular by Peter Behrens, who was in favour of building upwards in the business centre which was then being proposed.[55] More widely, the attention of many German architects had turned towards urban planning and the American skyscrapers. In 1914 Bruno Möhring proposed the construction of a high-rise building on a triangular site bordered by the River Spree, Friedrichstrasse and the Friedrichstrasse railway station. In 1920 he succeeded in inciting the professional bodies to put pressure on the Prussian Minister of the Interior to grant a dispensation from the height limit of 22 m (72′), and on 1 November 1922 the Turmhaus Aktiengesellschaft (Tower House Company), established for the purpose, launched a competition

THE FRIEDRICH-STRASSE SKYSCRAPER

[53] Paul Westheim, 'Mies van der Rohe, Entwicklung eines Architekten', loc. cit.

[54] Mies van der Rohe, letter to Walter Gropius, Berlin, 11 February 1919, Bauhaus-Archiv, Berlin.

[55] Peter Behrens, reply to a survey in the *Berliner Morgenpost*, 27 November 1912, and 'Einfluss von Zeit und Raumnutzung auf moderne Formentwicklung', in *Jahrbuch des Deutschen Werkbundes 1914*, Jena, Eugen Diederichs, 1914, p. 8 and following.

24

Opposite page: competition project for a Glass Skyscraper, Friedrichstrasse, Berlin, 1921, perspective of the whole building in charcoal (signed drawing, The Mies van der Rohe Archives, The Museum of Modern Art, New York).

Below: competition project for a Glass Skyscraper, Friedrichstrasse, Berlin, 1921, photomontage.

Competition project for a Glass Skyscraper, Friedrichstrasse, Berlin, 1921, charcoal elevation (signed drawing, The Mies van der Rohe Archive, Museum of Modern Art, New York).

Opposite page: project for a Glass Skyscraper, 1922, view of the model.

for a building 80 m (263') tall, comprising offices and a number of public facilities.

Among the great variety of projects submitted to the competition,[56] Mies's project, entitled 'Beehive', was distinguished for its avoidance of all reference to the context and of all visible hierarchical distinction between storeys with different functions. His entry resembles none of the others except that of his friend Hugo Häring. A triangular, steel-framed glass prism twenty storeys tall, with no definition of the base or the top, as though the roof had been sliced off, it occupied the whole of the triangular site. Three deep recesses afforded ground-floor access to the lifts, and allowed light to reach the three wings of the building, which were connected by a triangular central core. Mies gave an insight into his intentions in Bruno Taut's magazine, *Frühlicht*:

> ... a prismatic form corresponding to the triangle appeared to offer the right solution for this building, and I angled the respective facade fronts slightly toward each other to avoid the danger of an effect of lifelessness that often occurs if one employs large glass panels. My experiments with a glass model help me along the way and I soon recognized that by employing glass, it is not an effect of light and shadow one wants to achieve but a rich interplay of light reflections.[57]

This criticism of the effects of light and shade implies a breach with the architectural thinking of Behrens. Not only did Mies dispense with any differentiation between storeys; he entirely bypassed the problem of the articulation of the bearing elements and infills on the façade by using an unbroken glazed surface. No doubt an echo of the poems of Paul Scheerbart on 'Glass Architecture'[58] can be perceived in this great, undifferentiated prism. Francesco Dal Co and Manfredo Tafuri affirmed that 'the glass constructions of Mies distance the image of the town' and create 'impenetrable jewel-cases'; Hubert Damisch saw this as a far more complex, semiological statement.[59]

In the spring of 1922 Mies designed a second Glass Skyscraper, this time for an imaginary site, based on researches which extended the theme of the competition. Between the first and second versions the site becomes generalized, the lobby changes, and the outline becomes more freely sculptural. Carl Gotfrid stressed the 'dematerialization' and the 'timelessness' of

[56] Florian Zimmerman (editor), *Der Schrei nach dem Turmhaus, Der Ideen-wettbewerb Hochhaus am Bahnhof Friedrichstrasse Berlin 1921–1922*, Berlin, Argon-Verlag, 1988.

[57] Mies van der Rohe, 'Hochhäuser', *Frühlicht*, vol. 1, 1922, No. 4 p. 124. Translation: Fritz Neumeyer, *The Artless Word, Mies van der Rohe on the Building Art*, Cambridge (Mass.), London, MIT Press, 1991, p. 240.

[58] Paul Scheerbart, *Glasarchitektur*, Berlin, Der Sturm, 1914.

[59] Francesco Dal Co and Manfredo Tafuri, (*Architecture Contemporaine*), Paris, Gallimard/Electa, 1992, p. 129. Hubert Damisch, *Modern' Signe, Recherches sur le travail du signe dans l'architecture moderne*, Paris, Corda/CEHTA, 1977, vol. 2, p. 34.

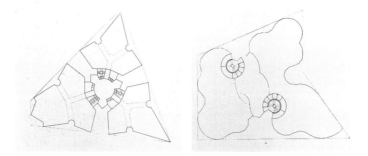

Comparison of the progression of floor plans between the projects for the Glass Skyscraper of 1921 and 1922.

Mies's two Glass Skyscrapers, animated by a sort of 'Gothic force'.[60] Mies himself insisted on the empirical character of his approach: the curves of the plan were the result of painstaking adjustment of the glass facets of the model on a plinth of modelling clay. Compared ironically by an early American critique to 'a nude building descending a staircase', the final outline does not (as was later alleged) bear any relation to the work of Hans Arp or the Expressionists:[61]

> At first glance the contour of the ground plan appears arbitrary, but in reality it is the result of many experiments on the glass model. The curves were determined by the need to illuminate the interior, the effect of the building mass in the urban context, and finally the play of the desired light reflection. Ground plan contours in which the curves were calculated from the point of view of light and shadow revealed themselves on the model, if glass was employed, as totally unsuitable. The only fixed points in the ground plan are the stairs and the elevator shafts.[62]

The second Glass Skyscraper design was related to the Berlin context in a model exhibited at the Grosse Berliner Kunstausstellung of 1923, showing a row of Berlin apartment houses, modelled in clay, at the feet of the transparent tower. This was more of a reference to traditional constructive systems and forms than it was a demonstration of the morphological adaptation of the project to the urban framework which it would reflect. Unlike the traditionalist skyscrapers envisaged by several German architects before 1914, Mies's two projects refer back to the glass structures that already existed in Berlin, such as the naves of Friedrichstrasse and Zoologischer Garten railway stations. They owe even more to these than they owe to Behrens's *Turbinenhalle* or to Gropius's and Meyer's Fagus factory. But the structure that supported these glass prisms, which were now vertical, was not explicit. The model was supported by posts with a circular section, but none of the floor plans clearly showed the configuration of the supports. If these cylindrical posts actually represented the proposed structure, their junction with the floor slabs remains decidedly mysterious.

[60] Carl Gotfrid, 'Hochhäuser', *Qualität*, vol. 3, Nos 5–12, August 1922–March 1923, pp. 63–66.

[61] 'Mies Speaks', loc. cit.

[62] Mies van der Rohe, 'Hochshäuser', loc. cit., Werner Gräff pointed out that Mies was afraid of the huge section of glass blinding passers-by and horses on the Friedrichstrasse: Werner Gräff, letter to Ludwig Glaeser, 6 July 1968, MoMA, quoted by Wolf Tegethoff, 'From Obscurity to Maturity: Mies van der Rohe's Breakthrough to Modernism', in Fritz Neumeyer, *The Artless Word*, op. cit., p. 240.

'Industrielles Bauen', article by Mies van der Rohe in *G*, June 1924.

G AND THE CONCRETE OFFICE BUILDING

This structural vagueness is all the more surprising, given that Mies's main grievance against 'Constructivist formalism' and the 'nebulous artistic indistinctness' of the organizers of the *Internationale Architekturausstellung* (International Architectural Exhibition) in Weimar in 1923 (at which he exhibited the model of the second Glass Skyscraper, which went missing on that occasion) was their acceptance of 'form in and for itself'.[63] Mies's new associations were indicated by his *rapprochement* with the De Stijl group, and his appearance in Berlin under the banner of the Novembergruppe. Affiliated to this organization, whose doctrinal radicalism was by now rather blunted, he came into contact with the core members of the Berlin Dada group – Raoul Hausmann, Hanna Höch and Kurt Schwitters – and with the founders of the short-lived Constructivist International – Hans Richter, El Lissitzky and Theo van Doesburg, who had all signed a common declaration at the International Congress of Progressive Artists in Düsseldorf in May 1922.[64]

In July 1923, Richter, Lissitzky and Werner Gräff, who had attended Van Doesburg's lectures at the Bauhaus, published the first issue of *G, Material für elementare Gestaltung*.[65] Like *L'Esprit Nouveau*, founded three years earlier, and like *Sovremennaya Arkhitektura*, three years later, this magazine presented images from the world of technology and deduced from them a scientific approach to architecture, rooted in the principle of economy and – in spite of the radical political views of Lissitzky and Richter – detached from any explicit connection with social reform. In its pages Mies settled some old scores, using a crossed-out image of a Bruno Paul house to affirm that the 'fundamental reorganisation of building trades is urgent'.[66] In its first issue, *G* published an article on the Concrete Office Building designed by Mies van der Rohe, and different in many ways from his previous tower blocks. The loss of the original model, which is known only from a bad photograph taken at the time of its presentation at Weimar in 1923, does not prevent the analysis of the structure of the building, which is fairly clear from a drawing – the original of which is almost 3 m (10′) in length. Two further drawings presented at the exhibition 'Les architectes du groupe De Stijl', which marked the first appearance of Mies's work in France,[67] have been lost.

The length of the building can be estimated only by assuming that the visible entrance is placed on an axis of symmetry. This

[63] Mies van der Rohe, letter to Werner Jakstein, 13 September 1923, LC, box 1. Translation: Fritz Neumeyer, *The Artless Word*, op. cit., p. 109.

[64] Published in *De Stijl*, No. 4, 1922, *KI, Konstruktivische Internationale schöpferische Arbeitsgemeinschaft 1922–1927, Utopien für eine europäische Kultur*, Stuttgart, Hatje, 1992.

[65] The write-up of the review was carried out in July 1923, at the time of the publication of issue No. 1, by Werner Gräff, El Lissitzky and Hans Richter. Mies van der Rohe, who would finance the publication out of his own pocket, joined from issue No. 2 in September 1923, and Friedrich Kiesler from issue No. 3 in June 1924. Two other issues followed, until April 1926. See the re-issue of all editions: Munich, Der Kern, 1986.

[66] *G*, No. 3, p. 13.

[67] It took place at the Léonce Rosenberg gallery from 15 October to 15 November 1923. Yve-Alain Bois, Jean-Paul Rayon, Bruno Reichlin, *De Stijl et l'architecture en France*, Paris, Institut français d'architecture, Liège, Pierre Mardaga, 1985.
  It was doubtless on this occasion that Charles de Noailles had the idea of asking Mies van der Rohe to build his house at Hyères, which was finally built by Mallet-Stevens.

Project for the Concrete
Office Building, 1922,
published in *G*, July
1923.

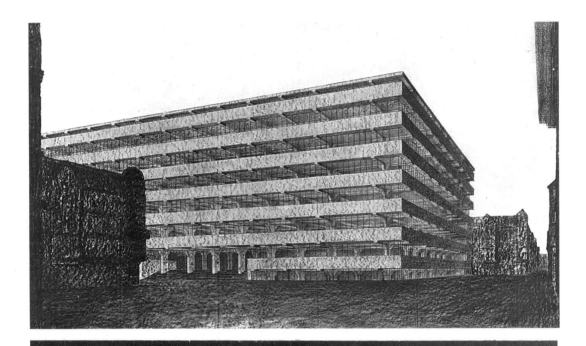

Jede ästhetische Spekulation,
jede Doktrin,   } lehnen wir ab.
und jeden Formalismus

Baukunst ist raumgefaßter Zeitwille.
Lebendig.   Wechselnd.   Neu.

Nicht das Gestern, nicht das Morgen, nur das Heute ist formbar.
Nur dieses Bauen gestaltet.

Gestaltet die Form aus dem Wesen der Aufgabe mit den
    Mitteln unserer Zeit.

                Das ist unsere Arbeit.

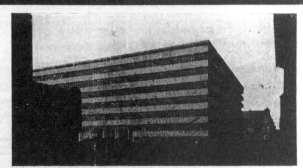

B Ü R O H A U S

Das Bürohaus ist ein Haus   der Arbeit   der Organisation   der Klarheit   der Ökonomie.
Helle weite Arbeitsräume, übersichtlich, ungeteilt, nur gegliedert wie der Organismus des Betriebes. Größter Effekt mit geringstem Auf-
wand an Mitteln.
    Die Materialien sind   Beton   Eisen   Glas.
    Eisenbetonbauten sind ihrem Wesen nach Skelettbauten. Keine Teigwaren   noch Panzertürme. Bei tragender Binderkon-
struktion eine nichttragende Wand. Also Haut- und Knochenbauten.
    Die zweckmäßigste Einteilung der Arbeitsplätze war für die Raumtiefe maßgebend; diese beträgt 16 m. Ein zweistieliger Rahmen
von 8 m Spannweite mit beiderseitiger Konsolauskragung von 4 m Länge wurde als das ökonomischste Konstruktionsprinzip ermittelt. Die
Binderentfernung beträgt 5 m. Dieses Bindersystem trägt die Deckenplatte, die am Ende der Kragarme senkrecht hochgewinkelt Außenhau
wird und als Rückwand der Regale dient, die aus dem Rauminnern der Übersichtlichkeit wegen in die Außenwände verlegt wurden. Übe
den 2 m hohen Regalen liegt ein bis zur Decke reichendes durchlaufendes Fensterband.
    Berlin, Mai 1923   Mies v. d. Roh

suggestion was put forward in 1969 by Ludwig Glaeser, who also hypothesized a central courtyard.[68] The floor slabs are supported by two sets of reinforced concrete columns, the clarity and rigour of which inspired Mies to affirm in *G* that they had nothing in common with the 'noodles' of contemporary office blocks in Berlin. The interaxis of the rows of columns is 5 m (16' 3"), with an unsupported span between the rows of 8 m (26' 3"), and a cantilever of 4 m (13') at each end. The building seems to float, being raised above the ground by a line of windows; by way of cornice, a slab, similar to the others, crowns a storey of reduced height. Each storey's perimeter enclosure consists of a solid wall to a height of at least 2 m (6' 6"), surmounted by a ribbon window which is set back, probably to shelter it from the rain.[69] There is no indication of internal partitioning, except in the entrance lobby, which is separated by a glass wall from the rest of the ground floor. Mies stressed the fact that the way in which the floor slabs turn up around the perimeter to become high parapet walls allows for the installation of a filing system under the windows, leaving the floors completely unobstructed.[70]

Unlike the two Glass Skyscrapers, which would afford their occupants views outside, this was a kind of *multi-storey factory*, faithfully expressing in this the determination of *G* to celebrate industrial objects and spaces as such. It is not inappropriate to compare this device based on a concrete framework with the Dom-ino House designed by Charles-Édouard Jeanneret in 1914, with which Mies was probably acquainted. The Dom-ino space is not subdivided inside, but is limited by the dimensions of the floor slabs and by the different infill components which at times block out the full height of the storey; the interior of the Concrete Office Building is completely open plan, and is sliced in two horizontally by the plane defined by the top of the parapet walls. Below this plane the expanse of offices stretches out, without a view to the outside; above is a swathe of air connecting the space to the outside with no interruption except the diaphragm of the windows. To accompany this scheme Mies produced a manifesto simply entitled *Bürohaus*, the first expression of his theoretical thinking:

> We reject any aesthetic speculation, any doctrine and any formalism. Building art is the spatially apprehended will of the epoch. Alive. Changing. New.[71]

In a longer text, written in July for the *Deutsche Allgemeine*

[68] Ludwig Glaeser, *Ludwig Mies van der Rohe; Drawings in the Collection of the Museum of Modern Art*, New York, MoMA, 1969.

[69] Wolf Tegethoff mentions a sunbreaker effect regarding this; see: 'From Obscurity to Maturity; Mies van der Rohe's Breakthrough to Modernism', op. cit., p. 50.

[70] Mies van der Rohe, 'Bürohaus', *G*, No. 1, July 1923, p. 3.

[71] Mies van der Rohe, 'Bürohaus', Translation: Fritz Neumeyer, *The Artless Word*, op. cit., p. 241.

[72] The newspaper received it too late for publishing: MoMA, manuscripts, file 3.

[73] Kurt Scheffler, *Moderne Baukunst*, Berlin, Julius Bard, 1907. Hermann Sörgel, *Architektur-Asthetik*, Munich, Piloty and Loeble, 1923, vol. 1. p. 256 and following.

[74] Peter Behrens, reply to a survey of the *Berliner Morgenpost*, loc. cit.

[75] Mies van der Rohe, 'Burohaus', manuscript, n.d., MoMA, box 3. Translation: Fritz Neumeyer, *The Artless Word*, op. cit., p. 241.

Zeitung,[72] he revealed the degree to which his architectural doctrine was rooted in the theories of the structural rationalists, from Viollet-le-Duc to Kurt Scheffler and Hermann Sörgel.[73] He had also considered the office work space, where Behrens had already envisaged in 1912 leaving whole floors of offices unpartitioned.[74]

> The office building illustrated here is a building of work, of organization, of clarity, of economy. Bright wide work-rooms, uncluttered, undivided, only articulated according to the organism of the firm. The greatest effect with the least expenditure of means. The materials are concrete, iron, glass. Ferroconcrete buildings are essentially skeleton structures. Neither noodles nor tank turrets. Supporting girder construction with a nonsupporting wall. That means skin and bone structures.[75]

THE CONCRETE COUNTRY HOUSE

[76] Mies van der Rohe, 'Bauen', loc. cit.

[77] Wolf Tegethoff, 'From Obscurity to Maturity: Mies van der Rohe's Breakthrough to Modernism', op. cit. pp. 52–53.

[78] This exhibition was organized by André Lurçat with the help of Van Doesburg: Jean-Louis Cohen, *André Lurçat (1894–1970): L'autocritique d'un moderne*, Paris, IFA, Liège, Piene Mandaga, 1995.

[79] Mies van der Rohe, conference of 19 June 1924, published by Fritz Neumeyer, *Mies van der Rohe, das Kunstlose Wort: Gedanken zur Baukunst*, op. cit., p. 309.

In the second issue of *G*, Mies published one of his most memorable texts, 'Bauen', in which he affirmed in particular that 'We know no forms, only problems of construction'.[76] This declaration accompanied a second exploration of the potential of reinforced concrete construction, which was also exhibited in the Berlin *Grosse Berliner Kunstausstellung* of May 1923. This was the Concrete Country House, which was in total contrast to his early domestic architectural work. A few metres away, Lissitzky exhibited his famous *Prounenraum*. The suggested setting for the house was Potsdam, and one might suppose that the eventual owner would be none other than the architect himself,[77] but the absence of context and explicit identification of the site made these aspects of secondary importance. Only the coloured charcoal drawings, probably made at a later date, and the photographs of the lost model which was the central feature of the project, remain. The plan and all the preparatory sketches have been lost, including the drawing shown by Van Doesburg at the Galerie de L'Effort Moderne in 1923 and at the Nancy-Paris exhibition of 1926.[78]

The Concrete Country House, like the Concrete Office Building, uses a column structure, but it does not have a regular framework. Thus, openings can be introduced at will – 'the skin forming both the roof and the walls', in Mies's words[79] – and the

Project for the Concrete
Country House, 1922,
perspective (signed
drawing, The Mies van
der Rohe Archive, The
Museum of Modern Art,
New York) and model.

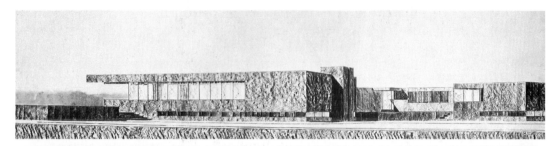

partitions positioned with total freedom. But, whereas the office
buildings are single units, the house by contrast spreads over the
ground, as if to cover and enclose as much of it as possible. The
main entrance is in the wall of the entrance courtyard, and is
marked by a flight of steps similar to that of the Concrete Office
Building and by a projecting canopy. It leads straight into an
entrance lobby, connected on the corner to a U recalling the 1914
project for the Mies house at Werder. One arm of the U leads to
the almost detached mass of the living-room, which is dominated
by a huge fireplace and lit by large horizontal windows; the other
contains one or more bedrooms. Both arms are linked together
by a large room of undefined purpose. The kitchen is in the
basement, accessible from the outside by a service entrance

marked by a canopy at the corner of the house. It is lit by a horizontal strip of windows similar to that of the ground floor of the Concrete Office Building.

The abstract appearance of the model from the photographs has led certain critics to see this design, no doubt incautiously, as a demonstration of 'self-referential' architecture, without precedence or referent.[80] In fact, the horizontal deployment of these rectilinear blocks reveals Mies's knowledge of the first *Proun* of Lissitzky, together with echoes of Wright's Prairie Houses. It is also noticeable that the divided plan of the house, unlike Wright's first solutions, lacks apparent hierarchical structure, and that the modelling of the platforms and floors recalls the layouts of the Wiegand and Kröller-Müller designs and can thus be related to the bases of the buildings of Schinkel. As for the precedents this house might have set, another remark is in order: the detached arrangement of its volumes is based on distinctions of function. This was the theme that Walter Gropius would develop explicitly in the Dessau Bauhaus of 1925.[81]

THE BRICK COUNTRY HOUSE

Situated this time, with no ambiguity, on a site near Neubabelsberg, which was well known to Mies and where he wanted to live himself, the Brick Country House was exhibited in the *Grosse Berliner Kunstausstellung* of 1924. Only the photographs survive of the two original drawings, which were a charcoal perspective drawn by Mies shortly before the opening of the exhibition and a plan, of which later versions appeared, with variations in the pattern of the brick fireplaces. The notable differences between the plan and the perspective no doubt indicate that the perspective was drawn earlier.[82] The plan is reminiscent both of the work seen at the Bauhaus exhibition at Weimar and of the work of De Stijl, a movement into which Mies had been hastily assimilated at the time of the exhibition at the Galerie de L'Effort Moderne.

The Brick Country House was precisely contemporary with the Mosler house, which demonstrates that Mies was quite at home using brickwork. It used the same material, but very different principles of composition, even though the Mosler house's cuboid kitchen gives an indication as to the appearance the building might have had. The vocabulary used in the Brick Country House consists of elementary forms, and associates brick walls of varying heights, two blocks each containing a fireplace, flat roofs with slight overhangs and vertical expanses of glass. The walls are

[80] Peter Eisenman 'Mies Reading . . .' in John Zukowsky (editor) *Mies Reconsidered: His career, Legacy and Disciples*, Chicago, Art Institute of Chicago, New York, Rizzoli, 1986, p. 92.

[81] Wolf Tegethoff, who submitted the most rigorous analysis of these plans, alluded to the correspondence between Gropius and Mies; see: *Mies van der Rohe; die Villen und Landhausprojekte*, op. cit., p. 32.

[82] Wolf Tegethoff, *Mies van der Rohe; die Villen und Landhausprojekte*, op. cit., p. 39. Mies denied this interpretation, stating that he had only wanted to spare the public from having to read through prints of the plans: 'Ludwig Mies van der Rohe', *Architectural Association Journal*, op. cit., p. 30.

Mosler house, Neubabelsberg, 1924, façade looking over the street and kitchen block (photos 1992).

screens which do not intersect but touch at their extremities. Mies stressed the contrast between this and the Concrete Country House:

> In the ground plan of this house, I have abandoned the usual concept of enclosed rooms and striven for a series of spatial effects rather than a row of individual rooms. The wall loses its enclosing character and serves only to articulate the house organism.[83]

Thus the space is fluid and continuous, inviting movement and offering a controlled openness to the landscape. The designs envisaged for the openings themselves remain mysterious, for they require lintels of a length 'incompatible with the structural possibilities of traditional brick', as Wolf Tegethoff has observed.[84] The function of the rooms is not specified, to the consternation of some of Mies's prospective clients, who asked him to 'put a name to the different spaces of the house'.[85] The plan is 'polarized' rather than centred on two zones of increased density; and this fundamentally distinguishes it from Theo van Doesburg's painting *Rhythms of a Russian Dance* (1918), with which it has (since 1936) been so frequently compared.[86] If there is any Russian dance involved, it is more likely to be that of the *Prouns* of Lissitzky, whose spatial development associates linear elements resembling the walls of a house with denser agglomerations. As for the relationship with De Stijl, this might be detected in Mies's expansion of the visual field of the rooms of the house, which is comparable with Piet Mondrian's ideas on the limits of his canvases.[87] On the other hand, the relationship between the fluidity of the interior spaces and the investigations of Frank Lloyd Wright is incontestable. Already obvious in the interior indeterminacy of the Concrete Office Building, which appears in the layout of the Larkin Building, this relationship is quite clear here. Moreover in 1940 Mies confessed that his debt to Wright dated back to 1910:

> At this moment, so critical for us, there came to Berlin the exhibition of the work of Frank Lloyd Wright. This comprehensive display and the extensive publication of his works enabled us really to become acquainted with the achievement of this architect. The encounter was destined to prove of great significance to the development of architecture in Europe.

[83] Mies van der Rohe, conference of 19 June 1924, published by Fritz Neumeyer, *Mies van der Rohe, das Kunstlose Wort: Gedanken zur Baukunst*, op. cit., p. 309. Translation: Fritz Neumeyer, *The Artless Word*, op. cit., p. 250.

[84] Wolf Tegethoff, *Mies van der Rohe; die Villen und Landhausprojekte*, op. cit. Translation: *Mies van der Rohe, The Villas and Country Houses*, New York, MoMA, Cambridge (Mass.), London, MIT Press, 1985, p. 16.

[85] Hans Berger, letter to Mies van der Rohe, Spittal, 14 January 1926, MoMA, general correspondence, file 2.

[86] Mies rejected this parallel, which was made in 1936: Alfred H. Barr, *Cubism and Abstract Art*, New York, MoMA, 1936, pp. 156–57.

[87] These convergences were mentioned by Hilberseimer: Ludwig Hilberseimer, *Mies van der Rohe*, Chicago, P. Theobald, 1956, p. 42.

1 and 3. Plans for the
Brick Country House,
Neubabelsberg, 1923,
perspective and plan.

2. El Lissitzky, *Proun*,
circa 1923, Busch-
Reisinger Museum,
Cambridge, Mass.

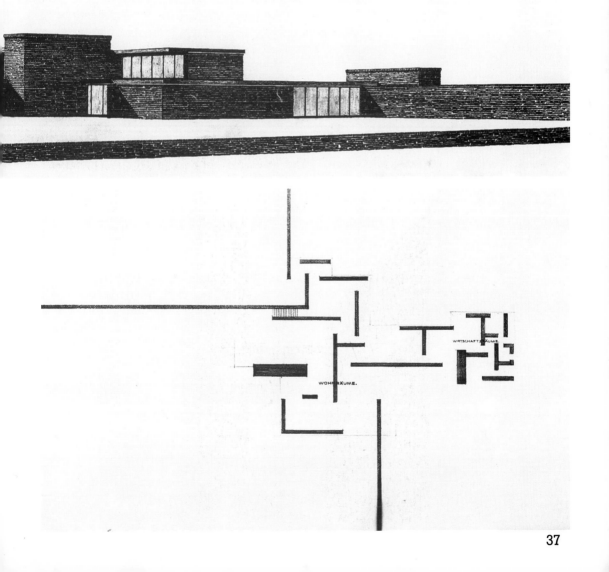

88 Mies van der Rohe, 'A Tribute to Frank Lloyd Wright', *College Art Journal*, vol VI, No. 1, autumn 1946, pp. 41–42. This text, written in 1940, was intended for a MoMA catalogue dedicated to Wright, which was not published. Fritz Neumeyer, *The Artless Word*, op. cit., p. 231.

89 'Mies van der Rohe, Gelöste Aufgaben; Eine Forderung an unser Bauwesen', *Bauwelt*, No. 52, 1923, p. 719.

90 Leo Frobenius, *Das unbekannte Afrika, Aufhellung der Schicksale eines Erdteils*, Munich, Beck, 1923. The echo of the Semper analyses is also noticeable: Gottfried Semper, *Der Stil in den technischen und tektonischen Künsten, oder praktische Asthetik*, Frankfurt/M., Verlag für Kunst und Wissenschaft, 1860–63.

91 Mies van der Rohe, 'Industrielles Bauen', *G*, No. 3, June 1924 pp. 11–13. Mies paid homage to Ford in his lecture of 19 June 1924, LC, box 61.

92 Fritz Neumeyer, *Mies van der Rohe, das Kunstlose Wort,: Gedanken zur Baukunst*, op. cit., pp. 100–2.

93 Mies van der Rohe, 'Baukunst und Zeitwille!', loc. cit., pp. 31–32. The illustrations provided by Mies for this text came from: Werner Lindner, *Die Ingenieurbauten in ihrer guten Gestaltung*, Berlin, Wasmuth, 1923. Translation: Fritz Neumeyer, *The Artless Word*, op. cit., p. 245.

The work of this great master revealed an architectural world of unexpected force and clarity of language, and also a disconcerting richness of form. Here finally was a master-builder drawing upon the veritable fountainhead of architecture, who with true originality lifted his architectural creations into the light. Here, again, at last, genuine organic architecture flowered.[88]

At this stage, almost fifteen years after leaving Behrens's office, Mies seems to have defined his own approach in terms of a personal synthesis of Schinkelesque and Wrightian experiments, reinterpreted in terms of the geometric networks explored by his own avant-garde contemporaries. He was now able to successfully elaborate a theoretical position that supplemented and expanded the previous comments that he had made on specific projects.

In his lecture in December 1923 on 'Resolved Problems', Mies stuck to the *G* line on the rejection of formal preoccupations and the exclusive concern with structure and materials, based on 'a new attitude towards construction', presenting as examples tepees, igloos and huts made out of branches.[89] This interest in the primitive dwelling did not come from reading Abbé Laugier, but from German geographers and anthropologists such as Leo Frobenius.[90] In a parallel article in *G*, he called for the industrialization of building, prophesying total prefabrication in factories, on the Ford model which the Germans found fascinating.[91] On a more theoretical level, his text of 1924, *Baukunst und Zeitwille!*, is an index of his own reading, which inclined towards medieval art history and popular science. Mies was particularly interested in the works of Raoul H. Francé on botany and natural harmony.[92] There are echoes of Oswald Spengler in this text; but the fact is that references, whether tacit or overt, to the *Decline of the West* are commonplace in all the architectural writing of the time, including that of the Russian Constructivists.

The Building Art is always the spatially apprehended will of the epoch, nothing else. Only when this simple truth is clearly recognized can the struggle for the principles of a new building art be conducted purposefully and effectively. Until then it must remain a chaos of confusing forces. For this reason the question as to the nature of the building art is of decisive importance. One will have to understand that all building art arises out of its own epoch and can only manifest itself in addressing vital tasks with the means of its own time. It has never been otherwise.[93]

Long before Spengler, such a view of the appropriateness of architecture to the themes of the age had been the central argument of Otto Wagner's little book *Moderne Architektur*, first published in 1896.[94] This argument was taken up by one of the founders of *G*, the Dadaist Hans Richter, who in 1925 attempted to profile the 'new master builder', who worked in a space which was 'internationally organized'; he expected of him a 'new sensuality' and the ability to respond to a society 'more practical and less sentimental', in a world of 'rapid mobility' and of 'precise calculation'.[95] There is no doubt that the real face of this *neue Baumeister* was none other than that of Ludwig Mies van der Rohe.

[94] Otto Wagner, *Moderne Architektur, seinen Schülern ein Führer auf diesem Kunstgebiete*, Vienna, A. Schroll, 1896.

[95] Hans Richter, 'Der neue Baumeister', *Qualitat*, vol. IV, No. 1–2 January–February 1925, pp. 3–9. Here Richter fundamentally opposes the *Baumeister* and the *Architekt*.

40

Foundations of a new domestic space (1925–30)

Recognized by the middle of the 1920s as one of the uncontested leaders of modern architecture, Mies van der Rohe plunged into his professional life. His commissions now gave him the freedom to abandon the language of conservatism to which previous clients had bound him and to which he was still bound with the Mosler house. He finally joined the Deutscher Werkbund, of which he became vice-president, and in April 1924 he founded the Ring, an organization intended to combat, in the name of the ideas of modern architecture, the unduly conservative Bund Deutscher Architekten (League of German Architects). Having been a member of the regional board of the Bund since 1923, he resigned with maximum publicity in 1926. He directed the activities of the Ring in close liaison with Hugo Häring, although doctrinally the two men were not at all close.[96]

His designs were not always built, although clients were now accepting the modern orientation of his architecture. The first client, in 1925, was the banker Walter Dexel, who was also director of the Kunstverein (Art Union) in Jena. Dexel had always encouraged the work of radical architects, but immediately quarrelled with Mies, who required delays which were in his opinion excessive.[97]

In the same year however Mies designed a house for the banker Ernst Eliat on a site at Nedlitz, near Potsdam. In this design he attempted to reconcile the principles of the Concrete Country House with the limitations of an actual programme, enclosing his sprawling plan within rather thick cement-block walls. In the only known perspective drawing,[98] the cuboid envelope of the house also reveals its affinities with Wright's Californian house designs, which were shown a few months earlier in *Wendingen*.

It was the house built in the small Silesian town of Guben for the industrialist Erich Wolf, who had been enthused by his visit to the Kempner house, that presented the first tangible evidence of Mies's new orientations. No photographic record survives of the interior of this building, which was built between 1925 and 1927 and destroyed during the Second World War. Mies located his house on the brow of the narrow site, which sloped down to the Neisse river. The ground floor opened on to a terrace. The plan developed the layout of the Eliat house, and the internal rooms clustered around this terrace without an enfilade. The front and street elevations were strongly emphasized by the contrast between the planes of brickwork, with the bond clearly visible, and the door and window openings. But seen from the bottom of

Opposite page: Erich Wolf house, Guben, 1925–27, views from the Neisse valley and from the terrace.

[95] Hans Richter, 'Der neue Baumeister', *Qualitat*, vol. IV, No. 1–2 January–February 1925, pp. 3–9. Here Richter fundamentally opposes the *Baumeister* and the *Architekt*.

[96] The signatures on the manifesto were those of Jürgen Bachmann, Otto Bartning, Peter Behrens, Otto Firle, Hugo Häring, Erich Mendelsohn, Mies, Hans Poelzig, Otto-Rudolf Salvisberg, Emil Schaudt, Walther Schildbach and Bruno Taut: communiqué of 26 April 1926, MoMA, associations, file 2.

[97] See the correspondence with the client: MoMA, small plans, file 2.

[98] Paul Westheim, 'Mies van der Rohe, Entwicklung eines Architekten', op. cit., p. 59.

Monument to Karl Liebknecht and Rosa Luxemburg, Friedrichsfelde cemetery, Berlin, 1926, general view.

Opposite page: View of the monument during a ceremony, published by the *Arbeiter Illustrierte Zeitung.*

the slope the outline of the house was partly obscured by the terrace wall – which was reminiscent of the Riehl house – so that it read almost as another horizontal layer, surmounting the retaining walls of the garden.

MIES AND WEIMAR POLITICS

[99] Paul Westheim, 'Das Haus eines Sammlers', *Der Kunstblatt*, No. 3, March 1926, pp. 106–13.

[100] Fuchs's (1870–1940) masterpiece, which gave rise to the nickname *Sittenfuchs* or 'Fox of manners', remains: *Illustrierte Sittengeschichte; vom Mittelalter bis zur Gegenwart* Munich, A. Langen, 1909–12. See also: Ulrich Weitz, *Salonkultur und Proletariat: Eduard Fuchs, Sammler, Sittengeschichtler,* Stuttgart, Stoeffler & Schuetz, 1991.

[101] Mies van der Rohe, letter to Donald Drew Egbert, 6 February 1951, quoted by Donald Drew Egbert, *Social Radicalism and the Arts; a Cultural History from the French Revolution to 1962,* Knopf, London, 1972, p. 662.

[102] Sergius Ruegenberg, 'Der Skelettbau ist keine Teigware', op. cit., p. 350.

[103] Mies van der Rohe, interview with Lisa Dechêne, *Deutsche Volkzeitung,* 5 September 1969, quoted by Rolf-Peter Baacke, Michael Nungesser, 'Ich bin, ich war, ich werde sein!' in *Wem gehört die Welt – Kunst und Gesellschaft in der Weimarer Republik* Berlin (West), NGBK, 1977, p. 287.

Mies van der Rohe continued his experiments with the architectural value of bricks when he received an unexpected commission for a monument in the Friedrichsfelde cemetery, Berlin, to commemorate the assassination of Karl Liebknecht and Rosa Luxemburg. In 1926 Mies met Eduard Fuchs, now the owner of the Perls house.[99] A former compositor, who had become manager of the Social Democrat newspaper *Vorwärts,* Fuchs had published several works on cultural history and sexual customs and possessed a considerable collection of etchings.[100] Horrified by the monument which was envisaged by the German Communist Party – far from being in sympathy with the Bolshevik ethos, he considered the proposal 'worthy of a banker' – Mies suggested to Fuchs that, in his opinion, 'as most of these people were shot in front of a brick wall, a brick wall would be what I would build as a monument'[101] – although according to Ruegenberg he had also considered using basalt blocks.[102] Fuchs secured him the commission, which he built in a few weeks with reject bricks whose coarse effect was in total contrast to the brickwork at Guben. The monument consisted of slabs of stretchers each with a course of headers at the bottom, with no thought of constructive realism: they were supported by a concrete core and steel rods. The large star placed in front of the blocks was made from steel components supplied by Krupp and welded together on site. Just as much as it was a monument – with an impressive frontal mass about 15 m (49') wide, underlined by shadows – this was a platform for oratory, which was used at important Communist demonstrations, in accordance with a symbolism which the 'Rhineland revolutionary' (as he called himself) was to recall forty years later:

> [I built it] in a square shape. I meant clarity and truth to join forces against the fog that had descended and was killing all hopes – the hopes, as we rightly perceived at the time, of a durable German republic.[103]

In his American exile Mies tried to imply that the commission for the monument had been fortuitous. The fact is, however, that in 1926 he also belonged to the Society of the Friends of New Russia,

WIR SIND NICHT ZU VERBIETEN! Von KARL LIEBKNECHT

Trotz Zörgiebels Gummiknüppelattacke, trotz aller Demonstrationsverbote erkämpfte sich die Berliner Arbeiterschaft die Straße, um in der Lenin-Liebknecht-Luxemburg-Woche für die Ideen ihrer großen Toten zu demonstrieren

Und wenn Ihr uns verboten habt,
Wir sind nicht zu bezwingen,
Wir regen doch, den Adlern gleich
Nur kräftiger die Schwingen.
Und habt Ihr uns auch tot gesagt,
Wir kämpfen weiter, unverzagt,
Wir sind nicht zu verbieten!

Wir sind der Sturm, wir sind die Glut!
Wir sind des Volkes Stimme.
Wir stürmen wie des Wassers Flut
Und trotzen Eurem Grimme!
Wir sind des Volkes Rachegeist,
Der Euch doch endlich niederreißt,
Wir sind nicht zu verbieten!

Rechts: An der Lichtensteinbrücke, von der Rosa Luxemburg in den Landwehrkanal geworfen wurde, legen die Arbeiter Kränze nieder

43

like his colleagues Bruno Taut and Erich Mendelsohn.[104] The friendship with Fuchs also brought him the commission of building an extension to the house he had built for Perls (who had been a friend of Liebknecht); Fuchs installed his etchings in the new wing in 1928. Committed, implicitly at any rate, on the side of the left, Mies nonetheless refused to take over Taut's position as city architect of Magdeburg in 1925, so as not to be entangled in party conflict.

As Richard Pommer has pointed out, his political orientation at that time approximated to that of the right wing of the German Democratic Party, which was generally favourable towards modern architecture;[105] he also drifted in an idealistic direction under the influence of the Quickborn (fountain of youth) movement, whose theoretician, the Catholic priest Romano Guardini, in his writings called for the irresistible power of industry to submit to an ideal force associating Plato and Nietzsche.[106] A new and more spiritual dimension thus began to appear in Mies's discourse, as he revealed, for example, in a lecture given in 1926:

> Building art (Baukunst) is not the realization of specific formal problems, no matter how much they may be contained therein. But it is always, I repeat, the spatial execution of spiritual decisions.[107]

The rather laboured assiduity with which Mies read the books of Guardini, of Friedrich Dessauer and of the Cologne architect Rudolf Schwarz on the philosophy of technology, is attested by his reading notes for the years 1927–28, which are now held at The Museum of Modern Art.[108] He remained on cordial terms with Schwarz, whose antifunctionalist modernism was never very similar to his own.[109] At that time Mies obtained his only commission for public housing (a flourishing sector in Weimar Germany). In Berlin, between late 1925 and 1927, he built four blocks of flats along Afrikanische Strasse, in the working class quarter of Wedding, for which he never subsequently showed much affection.[110]

This development is similar to certain contemporary projects of Bruno Taut, particularly because of the repetition of long blocks broken by standardized windows. They are austere in their ochre render and reasonably well equipped for cheap dwellings. The main blocks, which are aligned with the street, connect at each end to lower lateral wings, providing a pattern of autonomous and repetitive units, of which only the final one is distinguished by the inclusion of a shop. The slab blocks facing the street are joined

[104] The Society had sent him some documents concerning his activity since 1923, LC, box 2.

[105] Richard Pommer, 'Mies van der Rohe and the Political Ideology of the Modern Movement in Architecture', loc. cit.

[106] Romano Guardini, *Briefe vom Comer See*, Mayence, Mathias-Grünewald-Verlag, 1927 (these texts had already been published in 1923 and 1925 in *Schildgenossen*, a Quickborn magazine).

[107] Lecture dated 17 March 1926, published by Fritz Neumeyer, *Mies van der Rohe, das Kuntlose Wort: Gedanken zur Baukunst*, op. cit., p. 316. Translation: Fritz Neumeyer, *The Artless Word*, op. cit., p. 241.

[108] Friedrich Dessauer, *Philosophie der Technik*, Bonn, F. Cohen 1927. Mies van der Rohe, 17 March 1928, MoMA, manuscripts, file 1, n.p.

[109] Rudolf Schwarz, *Wegweisung der Technik*, Potsdam, Müller & Kipenheuer, 1928.

[110] In 1934, Mies refused to hand over the documentation concerning this complex for an RIBA exhibition. Mies van der Rohe, letter to RIBA, Berlin, 6 October 1934, LC.

45

Overall design of the housing complex of the Deutscher Werkbund at the Weissenhof, Stuttgart, 1927, model of the first version.

by their corners to the return wings, which look like separate cubes wearing loggias like masks, by three balconies, one above the other – the only curved elements in an otherwise orthogonal design.[111]

The experimental *Weissenhofsiedlung* in Stuttgart in 1927 was at the centre of European attention. Mies van der Rohe's appointment as director conferred on him the status of an organizer and urban planner, coupled with that of an innovator in collective housing, which Afrikanische Strasse would never have achieved for him. The Württemberg branch of the *Deutscher Werkbund* had been planning a national housing exhibition since 1925; Mies, now a vice-president of the *Werkbund*, found himself entrusted with the design of a show housing complex at the Weissenhof, a district overlooking the Swabian metropolis, which had been in process of being developed since 1920. His first sketch was ready at the end of 1925. At the top of the hill is a splash of cuboid houses, their crystallized flow following the hill's contour, and above them a cluster of apartment blocks form a sort of *Stadtkrone* (city crown). This design immediately aroused criticism from the most prominent local architects, who could not tolerate seeing this commission escape them. The traditionalist, Paul Schmitthenner, condemned Mies's plan for 'dilettantism', whereas Paul Bonatz reproached him for his 'romanticism'. In these circumstances Mies had to revise his plan in July 1926, imposing an almost orthogonal geometry, and simplifying the dominant verticals.[112]

In the final version of the overall project, the landscaping is greatly simplified. However, following the principles Mies used in his villas, it succeeds in unifying a development intended to accommodate 21 different buildings. Mies himself undertook the main apartment block and gave the other to Peter Behrens as an act of homage, asking him to add an edifice to those of a generation which he had helped to create. Relations between the invited architects, among whom were Gropius, Taut, Oud, Mart Stam, Hans Scharoun, Ludwig Hilberseimer and Le Corbusier, were hardly easy. The project was managed directly by Mies's Berlin office, with Richard Döcker acting as supervising job architect on site.[113]

The Mies apartment block dominates the development, with its four floors and four repeated units, each served by a stairwell leading to two flats per landing. For the first time, Mies used a steel frame; its stanchions at last permitted the openness and

[111] Fritz Neumeyer, 'Neues Bauen in Wedding', *Wedding im Wandel der Zeit*, Berlin, 1985, pp. 26–34.

[112] On the preparation, the construction and the echo of the estate, see: Karen Kirsch, *Die Weissenhofsiedlung: Werkbund-Austellung "Die Wohnung", Stuttgart 1927*, Stuttgart, Deutsche Verlags-Anstalt, 1987, and Christian Otto, Richard Pommer, *Weissenhof 1927 and the Modern Movement in Architecture*, Chicago, University of Chicago Press, 1991.

[113] The publications from the time are innumerable. Their references are given in the works quoted above.

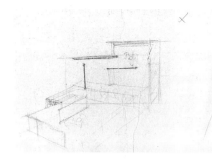

WERKBUNDAUSSTELLUNG
DIE **WOHNUNG**
STUTTGART
23. Juli bis 23. Oktober 1927

'Glass room' at the Deutscher Werkbund exhibition, Stuttgart, 1927, sketches of the design (signed drawing, The Mies van der Rohe Archive, The Museum of Modern Art, New York).

Catalogue cover from the Deutscher Werkbund exhibition, Stuttgart, 1927.

flexibility which had already been suggested by Behrens and to which Mies had long aspired. The framework is almost everywhere buried within the walls, although the variation in the layout of the flats reveals the potential freedom offered by this construction system. Mies carried out a demonstration by installing mobile partitions in certain flats, convinced that only the kitchens and the bathrooms should in the future remain fixed.[114] The joinery and the metal components evoke the world of industry, and the tubular chairs specially designed for the flats initiated a fruitful series of furniture. The exhibition inspired voluminous press comment in Germany and the rest of Europe; Mies's building was greeted with interest, being described by the trade paper *Deutsche Bauhütte* as a 'Bolshevik barracks'.

Away from the *Weissenhofsiedlung*, in the technical section of the Stuttgart exhibition, Mies built a 'glass room' – whose space was defined by partitions with different finishes and degrees of transparency; its tangential openings were a reversion to the Brick Country House of 1923. Basking in the public success of the exhibition, Mies took the opportunity offered by his numerous – and pithy – introductory texts in related publications to advance a new formulation of his theoretical position. He insisted on the importance of the spiritual dimension in new architecture, rejecting points of view which were 'unilateral and doctrinaire' concerning rationalization and standardization, but also attacking the idea of form 'as an end in itself'.[115] In this he seems to have been in agreement with Le Corbusier, whom he met in Stuttgart in 1926. Impressed by Le Corbusier's houses at the *Weissenhofsiedlung*, Mies called him to witness his own antifunctionalist position, which Le Corbusier – who was at that time in full cry against *Sachlichkeit* (objectivity) – could not but share:

> In Germany, a country of organisers, more particularly it seems to me necessary to underline with the greatest clarity that architecture cannot be reduced to crude functionalism. In Germany, the fight against the rationalists will be harder than the fight against the Academy.[116]

During the gestation process of the Stuttgart model development, Mies established a long-lasting relationship with Lilly Reich, an interior designer and fashion stylist trained by Josef Hoffmann; it was a relationship that was highly important in his professional and personal life. Lilly had known Mies since 1925 and had fully

[114] Mies van der Rohe, 'Zu meinem Block', *Bau und Wohnung*, Stuttgart, Julius Hoffmann, 1927, p. 77 (Deutscher Werkbund publication).

[115] Mies van der Rohe, 'Über die Form in der Architektur', *Die Form*, vol. 2, No. 2, 1927, p. 59; MoMA, manuscripts, file 6; preface to *Bau und Wohnung*, op. cit.

[116] Mies van der Rohe, letter to Le Corbusier, Berlin, 1 February 1929, FLC.

Show housing complex
of the Deutscher
Werkbund at the
Weissenhof, Stuttgart,
1927.

Opposite page: general
view; the interior of an
apartment in Mies's
building; Mies's
apartment
block in the housing
complex.

Left and below:
exterior views of Mies's
building.

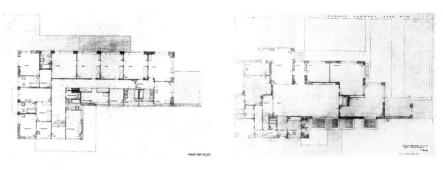

Joseph Esters house,
Krefeld, 1929, plan;
Hermann Lange house,
Krefeld, 1929, plan
(signed drawing, The
Mies van der Rohe
Archive, The Museum
of Modern Art, New
York).

Opposite page: Joseph
Esters house, view of
the garden elevation;
Hermann Lange house,
views from garden and
street elevations.

[117] The Lilly Reich
archives (Berlin 1885–1947)
are kept in MoMA, see:
Sonja Guenther, *Lilly Reich
Innenarchitektin,
Designerin,
Ausstellungsgestalterin*,
Stuttgart, Deutsche Verlags
Anstalt, 1988.

supported his candidature for the post of chief city planner in Frankfurt, which was finally given to Ernst May. She was to take part in many of his projects, in particular the interiors, exhibition design and furniture, and also for many years took charge of his daily life.[117] She introduced him to the industrialist Hermann Lange, owner of the Verseidag silk mills, who was to support Mies's work for ten years, after having entrusted him with the construction of his own house in Krefeld in the Ruhr (1927–30). To this commission was added one for the house next door, for Josef Esters, Lange's friend and joint shareholder. Mies seized this opportunity to renew the principles developed in the Wolf house, using an identical system of brick construction.

The two houses stand parallel to the street, their front doors being emphasized by overhangs. The strips of windows on their first floor show no regard for a strict correspondence between plan and elevation. The windows in the Lange house open on to a long corridor, whereas those of the Esters house light a series of separate rooms. On the garden side, the brick base of the Wolf house is repeated; more generous rectangular openings ensure the relationship with the interior, although by his own admission Mies would have liked 'to introduce a lot more glass into the house'.[118] There is a degree of contradiction between the openings and the fluidity of the ground floor rooms. This is not simply due to the use of a traditional structure: steel beams play an important role in complementing the load-bearing brick. Only recourse to a network of stanchions resolved this difficulty.[119]

THE BARCELONA FEAT

[118] 'Ludwig Mies van der
Rohe', *Architectural
Association Journal*, op. cit.,
p. 31.

[119] On the Lange house,
today a museum like the
Esters house, see: Walter
Cohen, 'Haus Lange in
Krefeld', *Museum der
Gegenwart*, vol. 1, No. 4,
first quarter of 1931, pp.
160–68.

After Stuttgart, Mies and Reich worked together for the fashion exhibition 'Die Mode der Dame', which took place in Berlin in the autumn of 1927, where they built the *Velvet and Silk* café, its spaces defined by textile screens and furnished with chairs from the *Weissenhofsiedlung*. They worked together again in 1929, in the German section of the International Exhibition in Barcelona. Hermann Lange was instrumental in the awarding of the commission to Mies for the whole of the German section, of which the centrepiece was a pavilion which was not intended, as has often been written, as a model dwelling, but as a place devised for and by the requirements of official ceremonies, in particular the formal reception for the King of Spain. It was nonetheless a turning

point in Mies's work and in the architecture of the twentieth
century. Its exegesis has been accompanied by a string of
clichés, which have been pertinently analysed by Juan Pablo
Bonta.[120] The scrupulous reconstruction of the pavilion, completed in 1986, has added a new dimension to the modern
perception of the building. The rediscovered colour seems rather
forced, because the pavilion has assumed the aura of authenticity
in the black and white of the photographs. To some extent this
reverses Walter Benjamin's thesis on 'the work of art in the era of
technical reproducibility'. However, the recreated opportunity of
passing through the space of the pavilion makes two-dimensional
reproductions pale by comparison.[121]

The pavilion was designed between November 1928 and
February 1929. After Mies's first sketches – now lost – a demountable model already showed two courtyards linked by a pavilion,
itself resembling a covered courtyard. The disjunction of the load-
bearing and space-dividing elements and the concentration on a
central core emerged in the course of the planning, although the
single roof and the strip open towards the street did not emerge
immediately. The preparatory drawings indicate the emphasis
that was placed on walls enclosing space, as well as the late
addition of eight metal columns. It was also only after several
attempts that the pool found its place in the corner. One of the
regulatory elements of the project was a single block of gold onyx
from the Atlas, which alone represented a fifth of the total cost; it
was bought by Mies himself during the winter of 1928 in Hamburg,
where it had been earmarked to make vases for a Norddeutsche
Lloyd ocean liner,[122] and sawn into slices 3 cm (1⅛") thick. In 1961
Mies asserted that the internal vertical dimensions were determined by the dimensions of these slices:

> When I had the idea for this building I had to look
> around. There was not much time, very little time in fact.
> It was deep in winter and you cannot move marble from
> the quarry in winter because it is still wet inside and
> would easily freeze to pieces. So we had to find dry
> material. I looked around in huge marble depots, and in
> one I found an onyx block. The block had a certain size
> and, since I had only the possibility of taking this block,
> I made the Pavilion twice that height.[123]

There was, however, no overall module determined by the onyx
block, any more than there was an overall grid – as can be seen·

[120] Juan Pablo Bonta,
*Anatomia de la
interpretación en
arquitectura*, Barcelona,
Gili, 1984.

[121] On the reconstruction,
already envisaged during
the 1950s as is shown in the
letters of Oriol Bohigas to
Mies (LC, box 20), see: *El
pavello alemany de
Barcelona de Mies van der
Rohe, 1929–1986*,
Barcelona, Fundacio
publica del pavello . . .,
1987.

[122] 'Mies speaks', loc. cit.,
p. 451.

[123] Mies van der Rohe,
comments collected by
Peter Carter, 'Mies van der
Rohe, An Appreciation on
the Occasion, this month, of
his 75th Birthday',
Architectural Design, vol.
31 No. 3, March 1961,
p. 100.

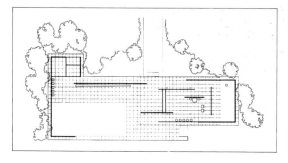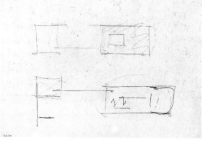

from the working drawings.[124] The grid appeared only in a drawing published by Werner Blaser in 1965. After a building process complicated by the difficulties encountered in stabilizing the slope, the pavilion offered a startling architectural journey from the entrance at foundation level through a reversal of direction into the interior, where the visitor came upon the dominant onyx wall, a jewel-box of stone that set off metal columns and glass partitions, one of which was internally lit, thus developing the theme of the *Glasraum* in Stuttgart.[125] Each interior space was matched, extended and echoed by an exterior space whose presence was all the more vital as no artificial lighting was installed. This essentially picturesque effect was to have been reinforced by the presence of several sculptures acting as perspectival focuses,[126] but the only one to be installed was the statue *Evening* by Georg Kolbe, to whom Mies had turned when he despaired of finding a work by his old friend Wilhelm Lehmbruck.

In this universe of transparencies and mineral and metal reflections, coloured planes stood out. The petrified landscape of the onyx wall set off the black carpet, and the red curtains framed the white leather chairs, designed for the King and Queen of Spain (who never sat on them). It must be noted that, if the vertical columns were accentuated by their stainless steel sheaths, the horizontal structure of the roof was played down to the point of giving the impression of being a homogeneous slab. In this unhierarchical space, open to diagonal views and to movement, the only perceptible symmetry was that which rendered the plane of the floor visually identical to that of the ceiling; there are certain photographs of the pavilion that can be viewed upside down.[127] This symmetry was of course revealed only once one had stepped up onto the plinth – another quotation from Schinkel. German officialdom seems to have recognized the qualities of the pavilion, as witness the appreciation voiced by the commissioner of the German delegation, Baron von Schnitzler:

> We have wanted to show here what we can do, what we are and how we feel today. We do not want anything more than clarity, simplicity and integrity.[128]

It is difficult to define what the policies of the German industrialists had in common with Mies's decision to present his slender steel columns as if they were precious objects – a civilized and

Opposite page: German pavilion at the International Exhibition in Barcelona, 1929, general view from the offices and interior view.

Above: German pavilion at the International Exhibition in Barcelona, 1929, final plan and design studies (signed drawing, The Mies van der Rohe Archive, The Museum of Modern Art, New York).

[124] *The Mies van der Rohe Archive*, op. cit., 1st section, vol. 2, drawing 14.22.

[125] José Quetglas, 'Fear of Glass', in Beatriz Colomina, K. Michael Hays (editors) *Architectureproduction*, Princeton, Princeton Architectural Press (Revisions 2), 1988.

[126] Caroline Constant, 'The Barcelona Pavilion as Landscape Garden: Modernity and the Picturesque', *AA Files*, No. 20, autumn 1990, pp. 46–54.

[127] Robin Evans, 'Mies van der Rohe's Paradoxical Symmetries', *AA Files*, No. 19, spring 1990, pp. 56–68.

[128] Quoted by Juan Pablo Bonta, *Anatomia de la interpretación en arquitectura*, op. cit., p. 60.

The 'Barcelona chair', 1929.

paradoxical echo of the skeletons of the African huts published in the books of Frobenius which Mies consulted, according to Sergius Ruegenberg.[129] After projects dominated by glass, with no explicit structure to speak of, such as the second Glass Skyscraper or the *Glasraum*, or by concrete and brick, the pavilion concentrated more on the theme of openness, which had already been explored in the Brick Country House, by introducing metal columns. Henceforth these were to delimit the interior of the building, liberating the vertical planes, which define the space, from the structure. The notion of the 'open plan' which Le Corbusier had formulated by the time he built his houses in Stuttgart,[130] and that of 'murality', extolled by Berlage, were thus solidly united.

The comments of certain of those who inspired the pavilion betrayed their lack of comprehension of this matter. Wright, to whom Mies was indebted for the opposition between the solid central core and the light precise structure, said 'Some day let's persuade Mies to get rid of those damned little steel posts that look so dangerous and interfering in his lovely designs.'[131] Mies, however, kept his columns in one of his families of designs, whereas the infinitely dilated space of the Pavilion of Electrical Industry, the most spectacular of numerous exhibitions put on with Lilly Reich in Barcelona, prefigured the family of large spaces free from supports.

[129] Sergius Ruegenberg, 'Der Skelettbau ist keine Teigware', op. cit., p. 347.

[130] The 'Five Points of a New Architecture', published in German in the Stuttgart catalogue had not escaped Mies's attention.

[131] Frank Lloyd Wright, letter to Philip Johnson, 26 February 1932, MoMA.

THE TUGENDHAT HOUSE

Designed while the Barcelona Pavilion was being built, the villa Tugendhat in Brno pursues the same architectural direction. The young American critic Philip Johnson told Oud of his admiration for this building in September 1930, when building work was almost completed:

> I wish I could communicate the feeling of seeing the Brünn House of Mies. I have only had similar architectural experiences before (at) the Hoek and in old things like the Parthenon. Of course such things should not be talked about because there enters into them so much that is extraneous, such as having studied Greek or being acquainted with the prophetic nature of Mies' own character. In American slang, the Brünn House is swell.[132]

[132] Philip Johnson, letter to J.J.P. Oud, 30 August 1931, MoMA Archives, New York, quoted in: Terence Riley, *The International Style: Exhibition 15 and the Museum of Modern Art*, New York, Rizzoli, 1992, p. 39.

German pavilion at the
International Exhibition
at Barcelona, 1929, view
of the patio with the
Georg Kolbe statue.

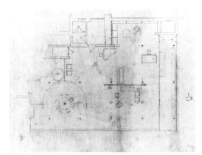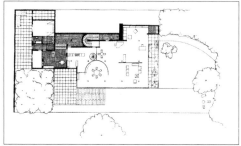

Fritz and Grete
Tugendhat house, Brno,
1929–30, plan detail
(signed drawing in The
Mies van der Rohe
Archive, The Museum
of Modern Art, New
York) and plan of the
main floor.

Opposite page: Fritz
and Grete Tugendhat
house, Brno, 1929–30,
view of the end wall
(photo 1991).

The recently married couple Grete and Fritz Tugendhat were friends of Eduard Fuchs. They were doubtless disappointed if they expected another Perls house. Contrary to the rather disparaging accounts that he liked to give of them afterwards, the Tugendhats seem to have fully committed themselves to the building of a house that was to unleash violent polemics even among the champions of *Neues Bauen*. The Tugendhat house is no minimal, reproducible house, like Le Corbusier's house in the *Weissenhofsiedlung* – with which, and with the villa Stein, it does show affinities – but a positively luxurious residence. This was more than some of the critics could bear.

In September 1928, when he was designing the Barcelona Pavilion, Mies went to inspect the Tugendhats' plot of ground at Black Field, overlooking the ancient Moravian city of Brno. It had been given to Grete Loew-Beer by her parents on the occasion of her marriage to Fritz Tugendhat. Both families were textile mill owners in an industrial centre where modern architecture had strongly taken root.[133] A close echo of the pavilion in Barcelona, the house was criticized in *Die Form* for being 'exhibition architecture'.[134] Certain components such as the onyx partition, the cruciform columns and the large plate-glass windows are identical, and several features of the plan echo the pavilion, such as the conservatory along the end wall of the building, in the position occupied in Barcelona by a small courtyard.[135] All in all the house is the more complex and the more dramatic of the two, because of the surprises it affords.

The slope of the land, accessed from the top and facing southwest, allowed the verticality of the three storey house to be concealed: only the upper floor is visible at street level. The opening between the garage and the bedrooms frames a view over the city, an indication of the importance of the view in the conception of the principal rooms of the house. From the entrance lobby, a staircase encased in frosted glass (or *Milchglas*) leads down to the reception rooms. Julius Posener drew attention to this arrangement, which is contrary to traditional rules, in that the path followed by guests cuts across the access route between the bedrooms and the living rooms.[136] From the foot of this staircase, the visitor sees the music room straight ahead and a view of the city diagonally ahead between a wooden cylindrical form on the right and the onyx partition on the left.

[133] On Brno: Vladimir
Šlapeta, *Die Brünner
Funktionalisten, Moderne
Architektur in Brno*,
Innsbruck, Technische
Fakultät der Universität
Innsbruck, 1985; on the
Tugendhat family, see:
Karel Menšik, Jaroslav
Vodička, *Vila Tugendhat
Brno*, Brno, Odbor vnitrich
veci Narodniho vyboru,
1986.

[134] Julius Bier, 'Kann man
im Haus Tugendhat
wohnen?', *Die Form*, vol. 6,
No. 10, 1931, pp. 392–93.

[135] On the house, see: Jan
Šapak, 'Vila Tugendhat',
Umeni, 1987, No. 1, pp. 167–
79.

[136] Julius Posener, 'Eine
Reise nach Brünn', *Bauwelt*,
vol. 60, 1969, No. 36, pp.
1244–45.

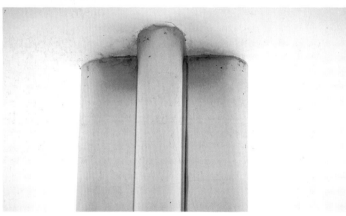

Fritz and Grete
Tugendhat house, Brno,
1929–30, overall view
from the garden; detail
of a column head; view
of the conservatory
(photos 1991).

Fritz and Greta
Tugendhat house, Brno,
1929–30, view of the
dining room in 1931; the
bedroom terrace; the
entrance (photos 1991).

The 'Brno chair'
1929–30.

The complexity of this large space reveals itself gradually. The degree of intimacy and visual protection increases from the glass wall on the valley side to the library area on the uphill side. The distance between the conservatory and the glass wall allows the making of an artificial landscape punctuated by slender columns – to the surprise of the Tugendhats, who had not understood the significance of the mysterious little crosses on their plans.[137] Internal columns are chrome-plated, their external counterparts are galvanized. The interplay between partitions, façades and vertical columns is more difficult and more complex than in Barcelona, because the main rooms are lit only on two sides. Inside the continuous glass wall, Mies defined the uses of his space by means of the sheltering palisander hemicylinder – which creates a conversation corner tucked in behind its outer face – and the onyx screen. The screen defines a living room which opens on to the conservatory and on to thin air, while restricting the outside view from the library area. The use of a curved form in this interior no doubt reflects Mies's interest in Le Corbusier's Villa Stein, a design that he had carefully studied. Fritz Tugendhat spoke of his pleasure in opening the great glass wall, which slid downward: 'In frosty weather, the lowered glass allows one to sit in the sun looking out over a snowy landscape, as at Davos.'[138]

Upstairs, the bedrooms line a well lit corridor. Like first-class cabins on a transatlantic liner, they open on to the upper terrace, a gangway in mid-air. The parents' suite of bedrooms and bathroom is mirrored by the children's suite.[139] The garden is divided into two parts – planted terraced beds and a lawn. It continues the stepped pattern of the house, in a manner reminiscent of the Wolf house. The size and comfort of the Tugendhat house, emphasized by Lilly Reich's decor and Mies's furniture (his third set of furniture, after Stuttgart and Barcelona) aroused reservations among critics linked to the Modern Movement; one of them, the Parisian Roger Ginsburger wrote an article in *Die Form* denouncing its 'luxury' as a travesty of the ideals of the *Neues Bauen*.[140]

In 1929 Mies further developed part of the spatial configuration of the Tugendhat house when he designed a house for the painter Emil Nolde in Zehlendorf, Berlin. He had met Nolde in the Riehl circle, and designed for him a single storey building, stretching out along solid unbroken walls on to which the living room

[137] Grete Tugendhat, 'Zum Bau des Hauses Tugendhat', *Bauwelt*, vol. 60, 1969, No. 36, pp. 1246–47.

[138] Fritz Tugendhat, 'Die Bewohner des Hauses Tugendhat äussern sich', *Die Form*, vol. 6, No. 11, 1931, p. 438.

[139] On the living conditions in the house see: Jan Šapak, 'Das Altagsleben in der Villa Tugendhat', *Werk/ Bauen + Wohnen*, 1988, No. 12, pp. 15–23.

[140] Roger Ginsburger and Walter Riezler, 'Zweckhaftigkeit und geistige Haltung', *Die Form*, vol. 6, No. 11, 1931, pp. 431–37.

[141] Curt Gravekamp, 'Mies van der Rohe: Glashaus in Berlin', *Das Kunstblatt*, No. 4, 1930, pp. 111–12. Wilhelm Lotz, 'Wettbewerb für ein Bürohaus am Hindenburgplatz in Stuttgart', *Die Form*, vol. 4. No. 6, 1929, pp. 151–53.

Adam Building,
Leipzigerstrasse, Berlin,
1928.

backed, as at Brno. But the commission was abandoned, and other, more ambitious projects responding to the problems of the German cities also came to nothing. In 1928 Mies returned to the office block programme with a design for a bank in Stuttgart and another for the Adam building, in Leipzigerstrasse in Berlin, abandoning the infill panels and the concrete structure to wrap the framework of the buildings in a wall of glass. In the Stuttgart building the wall supported trade signs and advertisements.[141] In the same year Martin Wagner launched a competition for the redevelopment of the Alexanderplatz, in Berlin, for which Mies composed a more complex metropolitan space, assembling his rectangular glass prisms according to a frontal logic, around the traffic roundabout which served as the central focus, and also according to a serial logic based on the repetition of six slabs of gradually increasing length. The competition was won by the Luckhardt brothers, but Ludwig Hilberseimer succeeded in reviving Mies's proposal as a topic of discussion.[142] In 1929 Mies returned to the triangular site in Friedrichstrasse with a design, which was once more unsuccessful, for a competition for an office block. The high rise of the Glass Skyscrapers of 1921–22 was abandoned, but the principle of the central core was retained, now solidly set at the heart of three glass-walled, concave wings. The building thus had three façades in which the disparate buildings of the area were reflected. The big city still remained closed to him, and so Mies van der Rohe responded to the call of the world of teaching.

[142] Ludwig Hilberseimer, 'Eine Würdigung des Projektes Mies van der Rohe für die Umbauung des Alexanderplatzes', *Das neue Berlin*, February 1929, pp. 39–40. See also: Paul Westheim, 'Umgestaltung des Alexanderplatzes', *Bauwelt*, vol. 20, No. 13, 1929, pp. 312–13.

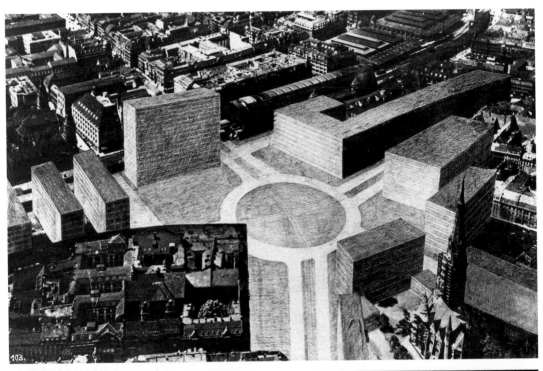

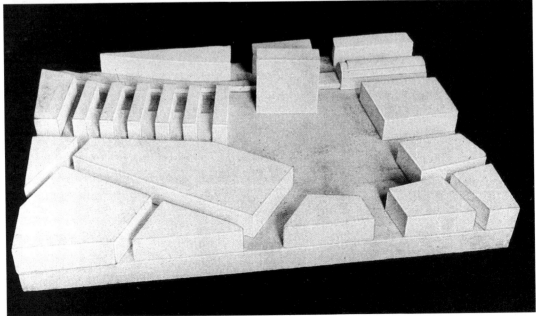

Competition project for
the layout of the
Alexanderplatz, Berlin,
1928, photomontage and
model of the design.

From the Bauhaus to the Third Reich (1930–38)

Mies van der Rohe's attitude in the first months of the Nazi régime was to lead Sybil Moholy-Nagy, thirty years later, to consider him a 'traitor'.[143] Again, Ise Gropius reproached him for supposedly supporting the régime, forgetting the efforts that Walter Gropius made to stay in Germany at precisely the time when Mies was involved in the Reichsbank competition.[144] What really was the relationship between Mies's career and German politics, during the decade at the end of which he left Europe? The directorship of the Bauhaus, held by Walter Gropius since its foundation in Weimar in 1919, was first offered to Mies in 1928, but in the event the post was taken by Hannes Meyer. Two years later, after Meyer had been driven from the post for political reasons,[145] Mies was visited in his office by a deputation consisting of Mayor Fritz Hesse of Dessau and Gropius, who told him that 'Without you it will crumble'.[146] He agreed to take the post. Philanthropic reasons seem, as it happens, to have counted for less than material ones, so slim were the economic prospects for Mies's practice in a Germany stricken by economic crisis, now that his work in Barcelona and Brno was finished, and his competition entries remained unproductive. He was appointed for five years on 5 August 1930.

The first encounter between Mies and his students was a disaster. The director called in the police to control the left-wing students, who were seething with resentment at the eviction of Meyer. Twenty of them were expelled. However, in a way Mies was only continuing the policies of his predecessor. Meyer had initiated a process intended to make the Bauhaus a true school of architecture. Mies pursued this aim by giving more weight to the teaching of Ludwig Hilberseimer, whom Meyer had enlisted to teach urban planning,[147] and of the photographer Walter Peterhans. He assigned the textile studio to Lilly Reich, to whom he also committed a large part of the school's administration. He emphasized the distinction between workshop activity and instruction within the Bauhaus, in order to concentrate on what constituted his first experience of teaching.[148]

The assignments that he gave to the students were limited in their scope. In particular he would require them to design courtyard houses, abandoning the collective housing projects of the Meyer era, and urging them to develop their designs through a long succession of sketches – up to a hundred of them – before making the finished drawings. The style of his corrections was

143 Sybil Moholy-Nagy, 'Modern Architecture Symposium', *Journal of the Society of Architectural Historians*, vol. 24, March 1965, pp. 83–84.

144 Richard Pommer, 'Mies van der Rohe and the Political Ideology of the Modern Movement in Architecture', op. cit., p. 98.

145 Claude Schnaidt, *Hannes Meyer: Bauten, Projekte und Schriften*, Teufen, A. Niggli, 1965. *Hannes Meyer, 1889–1954; Architekt, Urbanist, Lehrer*, Berlin, Ernst & Sohn, 1989.

146 Mies van der Rohe, 'The End of the Bauhaus', *Student Publications of the School of Design*, Raleigh, vol. 3, No. 3, spring 1953, p. 16.

147 On Hilberseimer, see: Marco De Michelis (editor), *Ludwig Hilberseimer 1885–1967, Rassegna*, No. 27, 1979; Richard Pommer (editor) *In the Shadow of Mies: Ludwig Hilberseimer, Architect, Educator and Urban Planner*, Chicago, the Art Institute, New York, Rizzoli, 1988.

148 Sandra Honey, 'Mies at the Bauhaus', *Architectural Association Quarterly*, vol. 10, No. 1, 1978, pp. 51–59.

Competition project for
a monument to the dead
inside Karl-Friedrich
Schinkel's Neue Wache,
Berlin, 1930. (Drawing,
The Mies van der Rohe
Archive, The Museum
of Modern Art, New
York.)

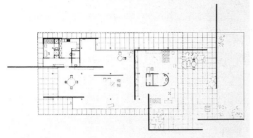
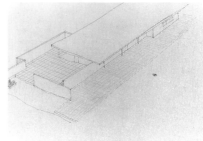

often curt, the Miesian *leitmotiv* being 'Start again!', as the American *Bauhausler* Howard Dearstyne tells us.[149] Gradually distancing himself from the heritage of Gropius and Meyer, he limited the scale and the complexity of acceptable plans, introducing into the Bauhaus studios correction techniques close to those used in his own office.

It was also in 1930 that he met Philip Johnson, who arrived in Berlin with his mother, his sister and his Cord convertible. He untiringly sought out the company of Mies and Lilly Reich, whom he took out for picnics, and commissioned the former to refurbish his apartment at 24 West 52nd Street, New York. Mies was ecstatic over the rationality of the floor plans of the apartment building and designed for the two-room apartment a fully demountable system of tables and shelves which could be transported over the Atlantic, and to which he added a selection of chairs from Barcelona and Brno.[150] Back in America, Johnson embarked on preparations for an exhibition of architecture for The Museum of Modern Art, and planned to entrust the exhibition design to Mies, who would also design a show house at the same time. In fact, in 1930, Johnson's apartment was practically Mies's only commission, as his two other projects were unsuccessful. One was the competition for the interior of the war memorial in Schinkel's Neue Wache building. Simply entitled *Raum* ('Space'), his design defined a large volume with Tinos marble walls, empty except for a thick black horizontal slab on the floor in its centre. The other project was a design for a golf club in Krefeld, which was very similar to that for the Nolde house.[151]

During these years, as the political atmosphere became more oppressive, Mies recorded his major success at the Building Exposition (*Bauausstellung*) in Berlin in 1931, which was held in a large exhibition hall. Mies, in charge of the section on contemporary dwellings, recruited the other participants, including Luckhardt, Häring, Gropius, Hilberseimer and Lilly Reich. He himself carried out a 'real construction project', a 'House for a Bachelor', in which the evolution of the theme of the Barcelona pavilion may be appreciated in direct relation to the subject of the dwelling.[152] The regular arrangement of metallic columns recalled the pavilion, but the walls which extended beyond the flat roof, opening out the internal space, were more reminiscent of the Brick Country House. The onyx partition also reappeared, but in the cylindrical form of the wooden screen in the Tugendhat

Opposite page: House for a Bachelor at the Berlin Building Exposition, Berlin, 1931.

Above: House for a Bachelor at the Berlin Building Exposition, plan and perspective (signed drawing, The Mies van der Rohe Archive, The Museum of Modern Art, New York).

[149] Howard Dearstyne, *Inside the Bauhaus*, New York, Rizzoli, 1986, p. 226.

[150] Philip Johnson, interview with the author, New York, 10 April 1991.

[151] Franz Schulze appeared sceptical as to his personal commitment in the project: *The Mies van der Rohe Archive*, op. cit., vol. 3, p. 52.

[152] Wilhelm Lotz, 'Die Halle II auf der Bauausstellung', *Die Form*, vol. 6, No. 7, 1931, pp. 341–49. 'Deutsche Bauausstellung Berlin 1931', *Der Baumeister*, vol. 29, No. 7, July 1931, pp. 261–68.

Karl Lemke house,
Berlin-Weissensee,
1932 (photos 1990).

house. One of the walls enclosing the dining-corner was made of glass and could slide down into the floor, like the windows in Brno and in the extension to the Henke house, which he had built in the previous year in Essen. There was no door between the living space and the two sleeping areas, which were separated by the block of the bathroom. The smaller of these looked out over a pool, at the edge of which stood a statue by Kolbe. Lilly Reich's house for a couple without children, in a more compact L-shape, was linked to Mies's house by a courtyard and used the same furniture. Reich also fitted out a flat in the collective building on *pilotis* which dominated the exhibition.

Shortly after this exhibition, Mies was invited by Herbert Gericke, the director of the German Academy in Rome, to take part in a competition to design the house he intended to build at Berlin-Wannsee. The design recalls the outline of the Brno house and especially, in the development of its ramifications from a central core, the projects of the early 1920s. The relationship with nature was fundamental: the whole living area, surrounded by floor-to-ceiling glass, was dominated by the landscape of the lake. By comparison with this ample and luxurious project, the one which Mies designed for the printer Karl Lemke on another lakeside site, on the shore of the Obersee in the Hohen-schönhausen district of Berlin, is fairly proletarian. This was actually built in 1932–33, the only executed project in a long series of designs for courtyard houses, and moreover remains practically intact.[153] Along with this very modest work, the only building of any size that Mies succeeded in building was the Verseidag factory at Krefeld, for his friends Lange and Esters. In 1930 he had received the commission for the dyeing works, which he effected in two parts between 1931 and 1935, combining a rigidly recti-linear slab with a low construction roofed by north lights. The tall building is constructed in encased steel. Its staircase, hidden in the angle of the walls, anticipates the designs used at the Illinois Institute of Technology ten years later.[154]

In the meantime, the Bauhaus situation had deteriorated. On 22 August 1932, the school was ejected from Dessau, where the town council, now dominated by the Nazis, had called in the spokes-man of the conservatives, Paul Schultze-Naumburg, to appraise the students' work. Mies agreed to confront Schultze-Naumburg publicly, convinced that he would succeed in convincing the Nazis of the apolitical nature of modern architecture. He also

[153] Situated at the heart of one of the zones of East Berlin long reserved for the Stasi, it became accessible in 1989. Volker Velter, 'Landhaus Lemke in Berlin-Hohenschönhausen', *Bauwelt*, No. 12, 1991, p. 536.

[154] Karl Otto Lüfkens, 'Die Verseidag-Bauten von Mies van der Rohe (1933 bis 1937), ein Dokument der Architektur des XX Jahrhunderts', *Die Heimat, Zeitschrift für niederrheinische Kultur-und-Heimatpflege*, vol. 48, December 1977, pp. 57–61. Wolf Tegethoff, 'Industriearchitektur und Neues Bauen, Mies van der Rohes Verseidag-Fabrik in Krefeld', *Architese*, No. 13, May-June 1983, pp. 33–38.

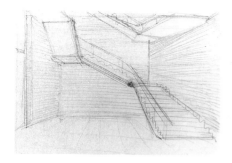 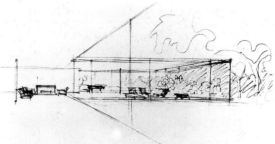

began to prepare himself for his survival under a future régime dominated by the Nazis.[155] When the Bauhaus reopened in Berlin-Steglitz on 25 October 1932, its status was no longer that of a public school, as it had been in Dessau, but of a private establishment owned by Mies, who advanced the 27 000 marks needed for the conversion of an old telephone factory building, 'less pretentious' and 'much better', he would say, than that by Gropius. In the move, he succeeded in eliminating student opposition to himself.[156]

It would not be long, as Mies told a *Bauhausler*, before the 'iron fist' that held Germany in its grip would crush the Bauhaus.[157] On 11 April 1933, little more than a month after the electoral victory of the Nazis, the police raided the Steglitz Bauhaus, under the pretext of a complaint from the authorities at Dessau. The students were taken in for questioning and the building sealed, but Mies had already evacuated the archives to Switzerland.[158] Against the advice of Reich and Hilberseimer, he went to plead with Alfred Rosenberg, whose Nazi party newspaper, the *Völkischer Beobachter*, had upheld the action of Schultze-Naumburg, and who was then in rivalry with Joseph Goebbels for the control of cultural policy. But this proved unproductive.[159]

Under pressure from right-wing students, led by Helmut Heide, who appealed to the *Kampfbund*, Mies went to the Gestapo in Berlin and met its head, Rudolph Diels, at the end of May. Diels had reservations about Kandinsky, a professor at the Bauhaus since 1922, but expressed no objection to the reopening of the school. The Dessau Nazis, who had launched the procedure, were apparently placated. On 20 July Mies received permission to resume teaching, under certain conditions imposed by the régime – notably the dismissal of Hilberseimer and Kandinsky. The faculty rejected the offer and the school was closed.

The Nazi policy of *Gleichschaltung* (or bringing in line) also applied to the Prussian Academy of Fine Arts, to which Mies had been admitted in 1931 in an attempt to co-opt the Modernists. Heinrich Mann and Käthe Kollwitz were forced out on 15 February 1933. Alfred Döblin and Martin Wagner protested and resigned, but Mies remained. On 1 July 1933, the Academy questioned Mies about his Aryan credentials. A few days earlier, a meeting of the association of Nazi students had praised the Modernists, including Mies. The exhibition which they had organized was closed. But Mies's professional situation was not in fact desperate: in July he

Factory for the Vereinigte Seidenwebereien AG, Krefeld, 1931–35, design sketch of the staircase (signed drawing, The Mies van der Rohe Archive, The Museum of Modern Art, New York).

Project for the Herbert Gericke house, Berlin-Wannsee, 1932, interior view (signed drawing, The Mies van der Rohe Archive, The Museum of Modern Art, New York).

[155] For this confrontation see: Mies van der Rohe, 'The End of the Bauhaus', op. cit., p. 16.

[156] For these episodes, see: Peter Hahn (editor), *Bauhaus Berlin* Weingarten, Kunstverein Weingarten, Berlin, Bauhaus-Archiv, 1985.

[157] Comments reported by Bertrand Goldberg, 'Kindergarten Plauderei', *Inland Architect*, March-April 1986, p. 28.

[158] Howard Dearstyne, *Inside the Bauhaus*, op. cit., p. 243.

[159] Mies van der Rohe, 'The End of the Bauhaus', op. cit., p. 16.

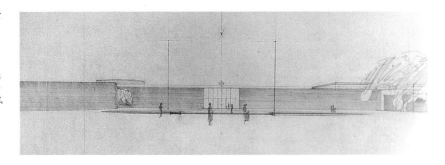

was invited to enter the final round of the competition for the Reichsbank head office; in the autumn he took part in the German representation at the Triennale in Milan, from which Gropius and Mendelsohn were excluded. On 1 September, at the Kulturtag (Culture Congress), Hitler combined a fierce criticism of the radical artistic tendencies which had flowered under the Weimar Republic with a degree of acceptance of what was called 'a functionalism of crystalline clarity'.[160] When Philip Johnson visited Germany that year he noted: 'there is only one man whom even the young men can defend and that is Mies van der Rohe'.[161]

There was indeed no lack of support for the Modernists. Goebbels gave their champion, Hans Weidemann, important duties for the Ministry of Propaganda, and he pressed Mies to design the 'Deutsches Volk – Deutsche Arbeit' ('German Nation – German Labour') exhibition and asked him to be part of the judging panel for the young artists' competition which he planned to launch for the *Kraft durch Freude* (Strength through Joy) organization. 'Deutsches Volk – Deutsche Arbeit' opened on 21 April 1934. Next to Gropius's contribution, Mies presented a section on mines, marked by the construction of two robust walls of coal and salt, delicately drawn – which Hitler disliked according to Albert Speer.[162] The situation was very unstable. Alfred Rosenberg took control of the *Kraft durch Freude* and sidelined Weidemann, while Hitler replaced the president of the Reichsbank, Hans Luther, with Hjalmar Schacht and cancelled the competition. These setbacks coincided with new attempts by Mies to bring himself closer to the régime. He had joined the *Reichskulturkammer* (Reich Chamber of Culture), and followed Schultze-Naumburg in signing a motion of support for the Führer on the occasion of the referendum of 19 August 1934,[163] no doubt because he feared becoming a 'second-class German', to quote Ivano Panaggi, who wondered whether this was 'necessity or ambition'.[164] Still full of illusions, Gropius himself had pondered, five months earlier, on the risks of seeing 'modern architecture and its spiritual leaders thrown overboard, when there is nothing to replace them'.[165] In January 1934 Gropius took part in the competition for the *Haus der Arbeit* (House of Labour), and later in the year he left Germany. Mies remained, and gave another of his minimalist indications of support for the régime by joining the *Volkswohlfahrt* (People's Welfare) on 30 August. His position was then considered to be secure by foreign observers. The Ameri-

[160] Adolf Hitler, *Die deutsche Kunst als stolzeste Verteidigung des deutschen Volkes*, Munich, 1934.

[161] Philip Johnson, 'Architecture in the Third Reich', *Hound and Horn*, vol. 7, No. 1, October–December 1933, pp. 137–39.

[162] Albert Speer, confidence shared with Elaine S. Hochmann on 29 July 1974; see *Architects of Fortune: Mies van der Rohe and the Third Reich*, op. cit., p. 213.

[163] Published in the *Volkischer Beobachter* on 18 August 1934, the names of Wilhelm Furtwängler, Georg Kolbe, Emil Nolde and Richard Strauss are also found here.

[164] Ivano Panaggi, letter to Walter Gropius, 25 August 1934, *Bauhaus Berlin*, op. cit., p. 226.

[165] Walter Gropius, letter to Eugen Hönig, 27 March 1934, quoted by Barbara Miller-Lane, *Architecture and Politics in Germany, 1918–1945*, Cambridge (Mass.), Harvard University Press, 1968, p. 181.

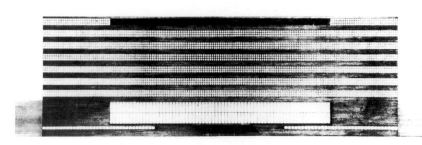

Competition project for the Reichsbank head office, Berlin, 1933, elevation.

can George Nelson supposed that he was the only Modernist to have any future;[166] but material – and financial – reality was more precarious.

Mies's great hope in the years 1933–34 had been the competition to design the Reichsbank building. His scheme was regulated by total axial symmetry, in contrast to all the neighbouring buildings. Its smooth eight-storey front façade traced a shallow curve similar to that of the Schocken department store built by Mendelsohn in Chemnitz in 1929, and afforded public access through a lobby 100 m (328′) long. At the rear the building presented a symmetrical composition of three wings to the River Spree. It retained the autonomy of the projects of the early twenties, but in a more monumental and rigorous vein.[167]

The sketch for the German pavilion at the 1935 exhibition in Brussels is closer to Mies's earlier approach. Presented as a representation of the 'essence of German labour' and surmounted by a Teutonic eagle of modest size, the project is in no way a renunciation of the principles of Barcelona; on the contrary, it extends them on a square plan within an opaque enclosure wall. But following Hitler's intervention, it was the monumental project by Ludwig Ruff which was chosen, before Germany finally withdrew altogether from the exhibition.[168] Another project by Mies, for a standardized Autobahn service station, also never saw the light of day.

Mies's preoccupation with courtyard houses at this time might be construed as a metaphor for the shrinking of his professional space. He developed ideas on this theme first conceived at the Bauhaus, his sketches introducing variants in the proportions of roofed parts and courtyards and in the scale of the living accommodation. This series was dominated by the House with Three Courts, for which he presented a perspective drawing in which a Braque reproduction indicated the material of a wall, and a house with a curved wall, in which the spatial tensions were the strongest. The pattern was now defined by blind enclosing walls, glass screens and slim metallic columns, often in rectilinear ensembles.

To this series were added two projects intended for real sites, neither of which was built. In 1935 he designed a house for Margaret Hubbe on the banks of the Elbe in Magdeburg, in which he repeated the theme of the courtyard houses in order, he said, to avoid a view which was 'boring, not to say annoying, towards

[166] 'Architecture of Europe Today: 7 – Van der Rohe (sic), Germany', *Pencil Points*, vol. 16, No. 9, September 1935, pp. 453–60.

[167] Friedrich Paulsen, 'Der Reichsbank-Wettbewerb', *Monatshefte für Baukunst und Städtebau*, vol. 17, 1933, pp. 337–44. 'Der Wettbewerb der Reichsbank', *Deutsche Bauzeitung*, vol. 67, No. 607, 14 August 1933, pp. 607–14.

[168] Richard Pommer, 'Mies van der Rohe and the Political Ideology of the Modern Movement in Architecture', op. cit., pp. 126–28.

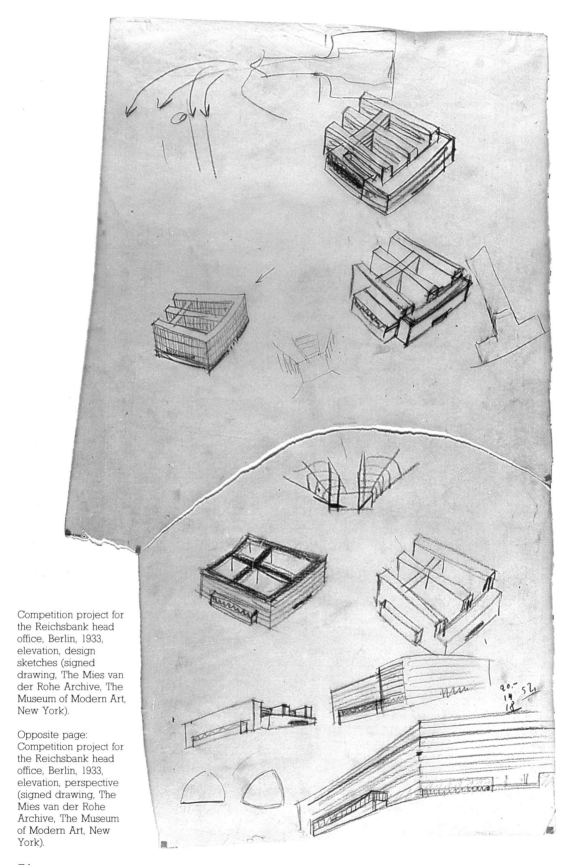

Competition project for the Reichsbank head office, Berlin, 1933, elevation, design sketches (signed drawing, The Mies van der Rohe Archive, The Museum of Modern Art, New York).

Opposite page: Competition project for the Reichsbank head office, Berlin, 1933, elevation, perspective (signed drawing, The Mies van der Rohe Archive, The Museum of Modern Art, New York).

74

Project for the Margaret
Hubbe house,
Magdeburg, 1935,
sketches of the interior
and plan.

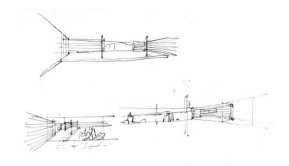

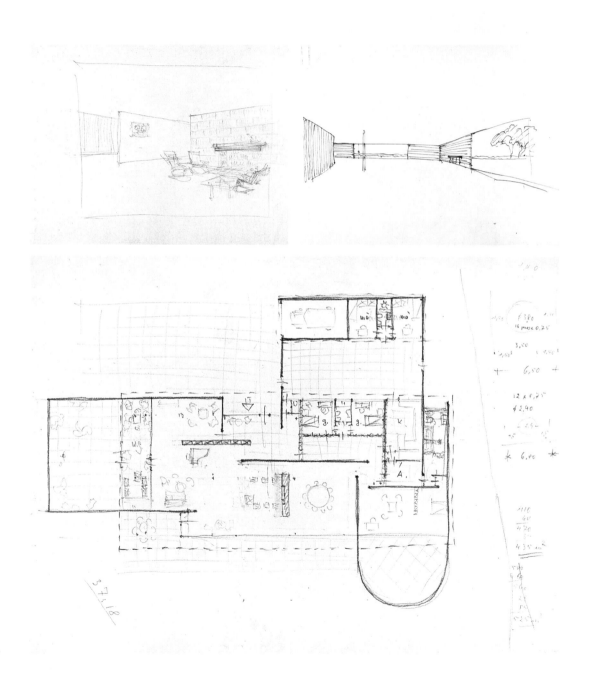

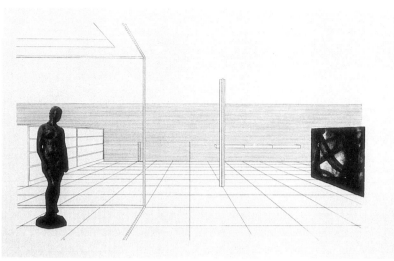

1. Interior perspective of a courtyard house.
2. Group of three houses, 1938.
3. Courtyard house with garage, 1934.
4. Ulrich Lange house, furnished plan and elevation (signed drawing, The Mies van der Rohe Archive, The Museum of Modern Art, New York).

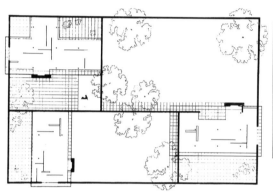

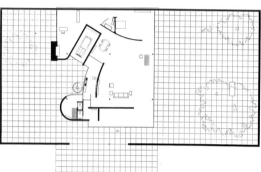

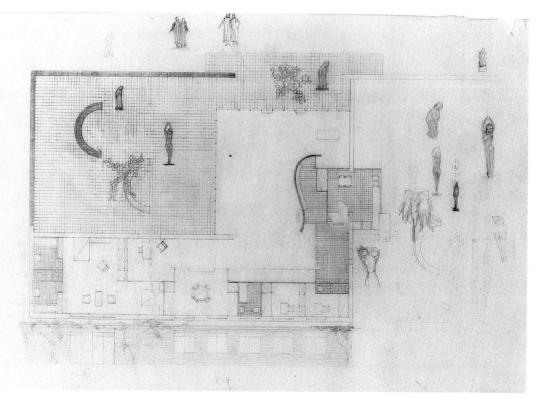

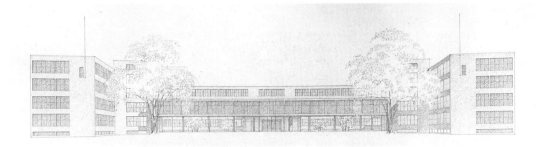

Project for an office building for the Vereinigte Seidenwebereien AG, Krefeld, 1937, perspective (signed drawing, The Mies van der Rohe Archive, The Museum of Modern Art, New York).

[169] Certain of these drawings, which occupy half of the fourth volume of *The Mies van der Rohe Archive* are analyzed in: Kurt W. Forster, 'Four Unpublished Drawings by Mies van der Rohe: a Commentary', *Res*, No. 16, autumn 1988, pp. 5–8.

[170] Bauhaus, letters to Philip Johnson, Dessau, 16 April 1931, 19 February and 1 September 1932, MoMA, correspondence with MoMA, file 1.

[171] Henry-Russell Hitchcock and Philip Johnson, *The International Style: Architecture since 1922*, New York, W.W. Norton, 1932. On the story of the exhibition and this book, about which Mies wrote to Johnson that it had given 'a good representation of the development of modern architecture in Europe', see: Terence Riley, *The International Style: Exhibition 15 and the Museum of Modern Art*, op. cit.

[172] Mies van der Rohe, letter to Philip Johnson, Berlin, 23 January 1934, MoMA, correspondence with the MoMA, file 1.

[173] John A. Holabird, letter to Mies van der Rohe, 20 March 1936, letter to John A. Holabird, 20 May 1936, LC.

the south'. He explored innumerable variations for a T-shaped building inside an enclosing wall opening towards the river. The house was not built, and the plot was sold. [169] The second project was a commission by the Langes for a house for their son Ulrich, in Krefeld. In the first version, the house was designed on one level, divided into two wings, one of them for services; later these were integrated into a single T-shape inside a brick wall. But the authorities rejected this project as 'un-German', although they then offered to accept it if it was surrounded by an earth bank; Mies refused, thus forfeiting the only tangible commission he had at the time.

In 1932, thanks to the active admiration of Philip Johnson, who had even proposed recruiting pupils for the Dessau Bauhaus, [170] Mies had been one of the stars of the exhibition of Modern architecture at The Museum of Modern Art, which proved popular in the United States. [171] An attempt by Johnson to mount an exhibition by Mies's pupils failed in the face of the latter's reservations, but there were numerous invitations to him to cross the Atlantic. [172] A first invitation to teach at Mills College in Oakland reached him in December 1935. After a month he turned it down, no doubt because of the new hopes aroused by the preparation of the German Textile Exhibition in 1937.

Celebrating his 50th birthday on 27 March 1936, Mies discussed with his friends an invitation from the Armour Institute in Chicago, and this time he did not close the door. [173] Shortly afterwards, on 20 June 1936, Alfred H. Barr suggested to him that he should work on the design of The Museum of Modern Art building, and that he should become the director of the Harvard School of Architecture. [174] Mies met Joseph Hudnut, Dean of the School, in August, but he was annoyed at being placed on a level with Gropius, who would eventually be appointed. Those close to him stressed every day the urgency of leaving Germany, where the situation was becoming increasingly difficult.

At the last moment the Textile Exhibition was placed under the patronage of Hermann Göring, who relieved Mies of his responsibilities and transferred them to Ernst Sagebiel, the architect of Tempelhof Airport. On 8 July 1937, the President of the Academy asked Mies to hand in his resignation, which he did on the 19th. Assured of the probability of an American commission, he arrived in New York on 20 August. He stayed until April 1938. He was shown round Chicago by John Barney Rodgers and two

Project for the
Stanley Resor house,
Jackson Hole,
Wyoming, 1937–38,
photomontage with a
Paul Klee painting.

former pupils of the Bauhaus, Bertrand Goldberg and William Priestley, and there he negotiated the post of director of the Armour Institute School of Architecture; and he travelled to Taliesin, Wisconsin, to meet Frank Lloyd Wright, before returning to Germany. He left his country for good after several weeks devoted to the final expression of confidence from Lange – a design for an administrative building for Verseidag – and without having been able to clinch the proposal for a Faculty of Law in Ankara, as Gestapo pressure became unendurable. He left behind him his family and Lilly Reich, who succeeded in conveying a large proportion of the archives of his office to a place of safety.[175]

In April 1938, the magazine *House and Garden* asked Mies for a design for the 'House of Tomorrow'.[176] But the American commission on which he concentrated was that for a holiday home at Jackson Hole in Wyoming for Mrs Stanley Resor, a trustee of MoMA, whom Barr had advised to approach Mies. The latter had met the Resors in Paris in 1937 and went to see their site, at the foot of the Grand Teton, during his first visit. In his designs (on which he worked until 1939) he had to take into account the foundations which had already been dug. While working he had in mind his own ideas formulated in the sketches of 1934 for a Glass House on a Hill. A large rectangle straddling a rushing stream with glazed walls facing up- and downstream, the house combined a steel frame with stone walls and a stone fireplace. The courtyard houses were forgotten, and the house opened up to magnificent views of the distant horizons, barely interrupted by the verticals of the columns, and framed by partitions. Nostalgic for a friend left behind in Europe, Mies pasted on one of the perspective montages, against the wide open spaces of the West, a reproduction of Paul Klee's painting *Bunte Mahlzeit* (1928).

[174] Alfred H. Barr, letter to Mies van der Rohe, 20 June 1936, MoMA.

[175] Lilly Reich visited Chicago in the summer of 1939, but she returned to Germany shortly before the war broke out.

[176] MoMA, general correspondence, 1930s, file 6.

Chicago and American paradigms (1938–56)

In 1937, Frank Lloyd Wright received Mies van der Rohe with more warmth than he had received any other European who had come to pay him homage – except perhaps Erich Mendelsohn in 1924 – a testimony to the admiration he felt for work for which he recognized that he himself had been an inspiration. Moreover, he agreed to introduce him on 18 October 1938, during a ceremonial dinner celebrating the nomination of Mies to the directorship of the Armour Institute's School of Architecture. This was partly in order to lay claim to his paternity:

> Ladies and gentlemen, *I* give you Mies van der Rohe. But for me there would have been no Mies – certainly none here tonight. I admire him as an architect and respect and love him as a man. Armour Institute, *I* give you my Mies van der Rohe. You treat him well and love him as I do, he will reward you.[177]

A month later, Mies wrote what was doubtless one of his last theoretical texts of any importance; in the American period his utterances became laconic and often repetitive in the extreme – except when he let himself go in evoking his memories. In this text he insisted on the importance of values 'anchored in the spiritual nature of man' for the teaching of architecture, alongside his 'practical objectives', repeating what the study of 'primitive' constructions or constructions in brick could teach. Concluding with the aphorism of Saint Augustine, 'Beauty is the splendor of Truth', which was constantly on his lips thereafter, he assembled the fruits of his reading of Simmel, Dessauer and Guardini into a definitive credo.

> Just as we acquainted ourselves with the materials and just as we must understand the nature of our goals, we must also learn about the spiritual position in which we stand. No cultural activity is possible otherwise; for also in these matters we must know what is, because we are dependent on the spirit of our time.
>
> Therefore we must come to understand the carrying and driving forces of our time. We must analyze their structure from the points of view of the material, the functional, and the spiritual.
>
> We must make it clear in what respects our epoch is similar to earlier ones and in what respects it differs.[178]

Opposite page: Metals and Minerals Research Building, Illinois Institute of Technology, Chicago, 1942–43, study sketch of the window (signed drawing, The Mies van der Rohe Archive, The Museum of Modern Art, New York).

[177] Frank Lloyd Wright, *An Autobiography*, New York, Duell, Sloan and Pearce, 1943, p. 429. Mies repaid Wright when in 1943 he signed his petition to the United States Government to organize the start of Broadacre City over the whole Union territory.

[178] Mies van der Rohe, inaugural speech as director of the ITT, 20 November 1938, manuscript, LC, published in: Fritz Neumeyer, *Mies van der Rohe, das Kunstlose Wort: Gedanken zur Baukunst*, op. cit., pp. 380–81. Translation: Fritz Neumeyer, *The Artless Word*, op. cit., p. 317.

Project for a Museum
for a Small City, 1942.

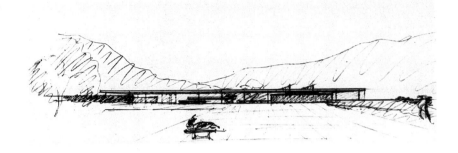

With the help of Rodgers and his colleagues from Dessau and Berlin, Hilberseimer and Peterhans, Mies totally reconstructed the curriculum at the Armour Institute; for the first three years he taught the first semesters himself, placing the emphasis almost exclusively on construction and drawing.[179]

> First we taught them how to draw. The first year is spent on that. And they learn how to draw. Then we taught them construction in stone, in brick, in wood, and made them learn something about engineering. We talked about concrete and steel. Then we taught them something about functions of buildings, and in the junior year we tried to teach them a sense of proportion and a sense of space. And only in the last year we came to a group of buildings. We don't teach them solutions, we teach them a way to solve problems.[180]

Progressively integrating his former students into a closed school, whose principles they would export into other universities, he guided his American students (who seem to have grown very tired of drawing endless brick walls) more and more towards two fundamental types: the courtyard house and the steel-framed tower.[181] Another frequent assignment was the design of a building which would have first a steel structure and then a wooden structure but would otherwise be identical. For the first few months Mies lived at the Blackstone Hotel, his Klee canvases stowed under his bed. He began a relationship with Lora Marx, whom he met on New Year's Eve in 1940, and this lasted until the end of a life that remained firmly rooted in the United States – he acquired citizenship in 1944. With the outbreak and spread of the war, Mies turned his back on Germany. At the time of the massive bombings of Germany by the Allies he even accepted the idea of his country being destroyed, if that was, as he said, the price to pay for ridding the world of a 'beast like Hitler'.[182] His horizons were confined to Chicago, a metropolis where the acceptance of culture and *design* by an élite limited to a few dozen now enabled him to reflect and act as he had never had the opportunity before. In 1939 Frank Lloyd Wright, who had suffered such hostility from a city which he nevertheless considered to be 'the greatest and most nearly beautiful city in our young nation',[183] paid tribute to the willingness of its industrialists to accept new forms:

[179] Stanley Tigerman, 'Mies van der Rohe, A Moral Modernist Model', *Perspecta*, No. 22, 1986, pp. 112–35. Werner Blaser, *Mies van der Rohe, Lehre und Schule*, Basle, Birkhäuser Verlag, 1981. Rolf Achilles, Kevin Harringotn and Charlotte Myrhum (editor) *Mies van der Rohe: Architect as Educator*, Chicago, The University of Chicago Press, 1986.

[180] Mies van der Rohe, interview with Peter Blake, *Four Great Makers of Modern Architecture*, New York, Columbia University, op. cit., p. 103.

[181] Edward Duckett and Joseph Fujikawa, in William S. Shell, *Impressions of Mies; an interview on Mies van der Rohe; his Early Chicago Years 1938–1948*, Chicago, 1988.

[182] Comments reported by Joseph Fujikawa, in William S. Shell, *Impressions of Mies; an Interview on Mies van der Rohe; his Early Chicago years 1938–1948*, op. cit., p. 29.

[183] Frank Lloyd Wright, *The Future of Architecture*, New York, The Horizon Press, 1953, p. 260, quoted by Hugh Dalziel Duncan, *Culture and Democracy; The Struggle for Form in Society and Architecture in Chicago and the Middle West during the Life and Times of Louis H. Sullivan*, Totowa, N.J., The Bedminster Press, 1965, p. xiv.

Project for a brick house, a student's work at the IIT.

To say that 'business' will some day know good architecture suited to its purpose, before art, science and education are able to recognize it, may be astonishing but, I believe, nevertheless, true ... The manufacturer, world over, in this has been a leader. Perhaps this is because 'culture', in quotation marks, had no place for it but in the final decisions of business – the mind of the superior businessman was more free than the pseudo-cultural academic to accept the change that is progress.[184]

The alliance of industrialists and businessmen had been at the origins of the First Chicago School. But Mies was not intimidated by the architecture of Louis Sullivan and the other members of that School. Later he rejected any suggestion that it had influenced him, declaring:

I really don't know the Chicago School. You see, I never walk. I always take taxis back and forth to work. I rarely see the city. In 1912 when I was working in The Hague I first saw a drawing by Louis Sullivan of one of his buildings. It interested me. Before I came to Chicago I also knew about Frank Lloyd Wright and particularly about the Robie House.[185]

He claimed that he had not changed in any way by living in Chicago, a city whose affinities with Berlin had been stressed by a number of observers at the turn of the century. Mies admitted no more than a vague interest in Marshall Field H.H. Richardson's warehouse, which had been demolished in 1935.

Two projects marked the turning point between the issues of the 1930s and the new American perspective. In 1942, at the request of *Architectural Record*, Mies produced theoretical designs for a 'Museum for a Small City', extending some work done with one of his students, George Danforth; in this the play of horizontal and vertical planes within the rooms reappears, as does the enclosure wall. The columns have virtually disappeared, as has any reference to the distant landscape (which was still an important feature of the Resor house). The interplay of partitions and isolated objects is illustrated by a collage, the most striking feature of which is a reproduction of Picasso's *Guernica*, a parallel

[184] *Frank Lloyd Wright, The Living City*, New York, The Horizon Press, 1958, p. 164, quoted by Hugh Dalziel Duncan, *Culture and Democracy*, op. cit., p. xiv.

[185] Comments reported by Katharine Kuh, 'Mies van der Rohe: Modern Classicist', *Saturday Review of Literature*, 23 January 1965, p. 61.

Project for the Stanley Resor house, Jackson Hole, Wyoming, 1937–38, view of the landscape from the interior.

186 Myron Goldsmith told Jordy of Mies's interest in Kahn: William H. Jordy, *American Buildings and their Architects*, vol. 4, Garden City, N.Y., Anchor Press, 1976, p. 224. On the multiform work of Albert Kahn Associates see: George Nelson, *Industrial Architecture of Albert Kahn Inc.*, New York, Architectural Book Publishing Co, 1939. The factory features in this on page 38.

187 Later, Paepke set up, with Robert H. Hutchins and Mortimer J. Adler, the Aspen Institute for Humanistic Studies: James Sloane Allen, *The Romance of Commerce and Culture; Capitalism, Modernism and the Chicago-Aspen Crusade for Cultural Reform*, Chicago/London, The University of Chicago Press, 1969, 1983.

188 Harold M. Mayer, Richard C. Wade, *Chicago: Growth of a Metropolis*, Chicago/London, The University of Chicago Press, 1969, p. 375 and following.

189 'Ludwig Mies van der Rohe', *Architectural Association Journal*, op. cit., p. 35.

190 Henry T. Heald, in *Four Great Makers of Modern Architecture*, New York, Columbia University, op. cit., pp. 105–8. An engineer, Henry Townley Heald (1904–75) was president of the IIT from 1940 to 1952.

to the savagery of the Nazi war. The contemporary Concert Hall project also utilizes a collage, in which the horizontal and vertical planes are no longer defined by low courtyard walls, or even by mountainous horizons. The elements defining the space of the hall have been stuck on to a photograph of the roof trusses of the Glenn Martin bomber factory, built in Baltimore by the industrial architect Albert Kahn and which Mies had found in a publication.[186] This juxtaposition might be interpreted as Mies's gesture of approval of the American war effort. In my opinion, however, it owes more to the great works of engineering publicized before 1914 by the Werkbund publications, in which Mies found all the scope – real rather than metaphorical – and potential for his own work.

Chicago was undoubtedly one place where the alliance between industrialists and architects, so fervently demanded by the Werkbund, stood out the most clearly. After the brief moment of optimism which the exhibition of 1933–34, *A Century of Progress*, had represented in the midst of the Depression, the influx of European émigrés was looked upon favourably by the president of the Container Corporation of America, Walter Paul Paepke, who supported the establishment in September 1937 of the New Bauhaus by László Moholy-Nagy.[187] Mies himself enjoyed the support both of Wright and of the profession at large, in the person of Holabird, but it was at IIT that he discovered the industrial world. The Illinois Institute of Technology (IIT) was created in 1940 from the amalgamation of the Armour and Lewis Institutes. From his arrival, alongside the reorganization of the school of architecture at the Armour Institute, Mies worked with Ludwig Hilberseimer on a site plan for the new IIT campus, which was to be inserted into the clearance and redevelopment of the insalubrious districts of the Near South Side, where the brick building of the Armour Institute had stood since 1901, and from which the black population was now expelled. A total of 60 km^2 [23 square miles] of slums were razed in this area under the Master Plan of Residential Land Use of 1943.[188] The president of the Institute, Henry T. Heald, was unsparing in his support, being enthused by the idea of creating a real campus[189] and going as far as to turn down a donation that stipulated the construction of a Gothic building. He defended Mies in the face of resistance from the architectural faculty (which existed in a permanent state of frustration in an institution dominated by research centres financed by industry and the military).[190]

Project for the
Stanley Resor house,
Jackson Hole,
Wyoming, 1937–38,
model.

Project for a Museum
for a Small City, 1942,
interior,
photomontage.

Project for a Concert
Hall, 1942, interior,
photomontage.

Design of the campus
layout, Illinois
Institute of
Technology,
Chicago, 1940–41,
aerial view and plan
of the first scheme
(signed drawing, The
Mies van der Rohe
Archive, The
Museum of Modern
Art, New York).

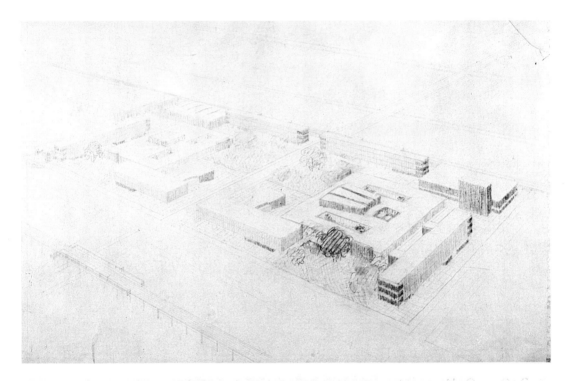

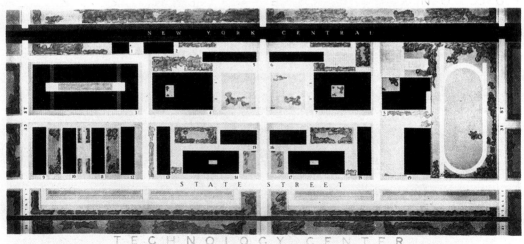

1. POWER HOUSE
2. METALS RESEARCH
3. ENGINEERING RESEARCH
4. AUDITORIUM AND STUDENT UNION
5. ELECTRICAL ENGINEERING
6. CIVIL ENGINEERING
7. LIBRARY AND ADMINISTRATION

8. GYMNASIUM AND NATATORIUM
9. INSTITUTE OF GAS TECHNOLOGY
10. LITHOGRAPHIC TECHNICAL FOUNDATION
11. RESEARCH LABORATORY
12. ARMOUR RESEARCH FOUNDATION
13. HUMANITIES
14. MECHANICAL ENGINEERING

15. ARCHITECTURE AND APPLIED ARTS
16. CHEMISTRY
17. METALLURGY AND CHEMICAL ENGINEERING
18. MILITARY TACTICS
19. FIELDHOUSE
20. ATHLETIC FIELD

Metals and Minerals Research Building, Illinois Institute of Technology, Chicago, 1942–43, East façade (photo 1993).

The initial plan envisaged the construction of 20 buildings on a rectangular site aligned with 33rd Street, to the south of the city centre and crossed by a fixed layout grid of 24 × 24 feet [7.3 × 7.3 m] (horizontal) × 12 feet [3.7 m] (vertical). Mies built 22 buildings in all, on a principle which Joseph Rykwert described in 1949 as 'slick and lucid', but also 'sickening', condemning the 'violent change in attitude' that had come upon him since the 1930s.[191] Before IIT terminated the commission on his retirement from the school in 1958, he worked mostly with Chicago architectural firms that dealt with technical design and problems of fluid engineering, which were particularly significant here. IIT managed to construct only two buildings before 1945; but after the war, having become extremely prosperous thanks to subsidized industrial and military research, it began work on others one by one. The picture given by the photographs is that of an ensemble of industrial buildings rather similar to those which Herbert Rimpl or Ernst Neufert, modern architects integrated into Nazi industrial and military policy, had constructed after 1933. Combining brick-work and steel frame in varied configurations, Mies for his part built the dimension of time into the whole enterprise, confident that the initial principles would not become obsolete:

> I was not afraid of that. The concept would not become outmoded for two reasons. It is radical and conservative at once. It is radical in accepting the scientific and technological driving and sustaining forces of our time. It has a scientific character, but it is not science. It uses technological means but it is not technology. It is conservative as it is not only concerned with a purpose but also with a meaning, as it is not only concerned with a function but also with an expression. It is conservative as it is based on the eternal laws of architecture: Order, Space, Proportion.[192]

Only nine laboratory and dormitory buildings resort to a concrete skeleton, with brick infill. Elsewhere Mies propounds his interpretation of the Chicago experiments in steel frame construction, developing a very precise grammar of steel sheets and profiles. The Metals and Minerals Research Building (1941–42), on the edge of the campus, was the first to be built. Anchored on a high brick base and lit by small windows, it recycled second hand materials and tools.[193] Mies worked with a consummate elegance.

[191] Joseph Rykwert, 'Mies van der Rohe', Burlington, vol. 91, September 1949, p. 269.

[192] Mies van der Rohe, comments collected by Peter Carter, op. cit., p. 206.

[193] Mies van der Rohe, interview with Peter Blake, op. cit., pp. 101–2.

Alumni Memorial
Hall, Illinois Institute
of Technology,
Chicago, 1945–46,
one of the two
staircases (photo
1993).

Opposite page:
Project for the
Library and
Administration
building, Illinois
Institute of
Technology,
Chicago, 1944–45,
sketch of the corner
(signed drawing, The
Mies van der Rohe
Archive, The

Museum of Modern
Art, New York).

Alumni Memorial
Hall, Illinois Institute
of Technology,
Chicago, 1945–46,
view of the corner.

Its exposed internal structure is its most noticeable characteristic.[194] Afterwards, Mies designed highly repetitive buildings, in which the spatial organization hardly varies, and also unique buildings such as the library and administration block, a large rectilinear slab 100 m (328') long, with glass panels that would have been the largest in America. This building, which was never built, would have signified on campus the symbolic and actual pre-eminence of reading and study.

The first post-war building at IIT was the Alumni Memorial Hall, dedicated to former students who had fallen in the war, for which Mies used glass panels opposite smaller, solid wall units. The staircases, tucked in between two brick walls and lit by golden light from the high windows, introduce a kind of mystery into the building, where the spirit of Schinkel meets with echoes of the staircases in the Fagus factory by Gropius and Meyer. Moreover, the detailing of the recessed joint between the rolled steel profile that forms the corner of the building and the brickwork of the wall is strongly reminiscent of Schinkel's Altes Museum. It celebrates the external clarity of the metal skeleton; its sturdy base plate emphasizes its firm footing in the ground and the recessed joint expresses its separateness from the brick infill. In this complex array of buildings based on common structural principles, the boiler plant (1949–50) and the chapel (1952) – a rectilinear box sliced into five bays and furnished in the most spartan way, its proportions recalling those of Schinkel's Neue Wache – stand out by their sheer mass and their distinctive treatment. On the east of the campus Mies also built a series of dormitory buildings in reinforced concrete.

In 1945 Mies at last had the opportunity to return to the domestic scale, with a commission from the kidney specialist Dr Edith Farnsworth, to whom The Museum of Modern Art had recommended him. Drawn to him by an initial liking that seems to have been mutual, she asked him to design a rural hideaway on a site beside the Fox River, 80 km (50 miles) west of Chicago. On this large wooded plot, 4 hectares (20 acres) in area, Mies built his first house in 15 years. It is very different in principle from the courtyard houses of the 1930s and from his earlier houses. He was to admit that the work had been made 'easier' for him because of the fact that it concerned a 'single person'[195] and a site surrounded by private land which ensured privacy.

[194] 'Metals and Minerals Research Building, Illinois Institute of Technology', *The Architectural Forum*, vol. 79, No. 5, November 1943, pp. 88–90.

[195] Mies van der Rohe, interview for the BBC, May 1959, quoted by Wolf Tegethoff, *Mies van der Rohe; die Villen und Landhausprojekte*, op. cit., p. 131.

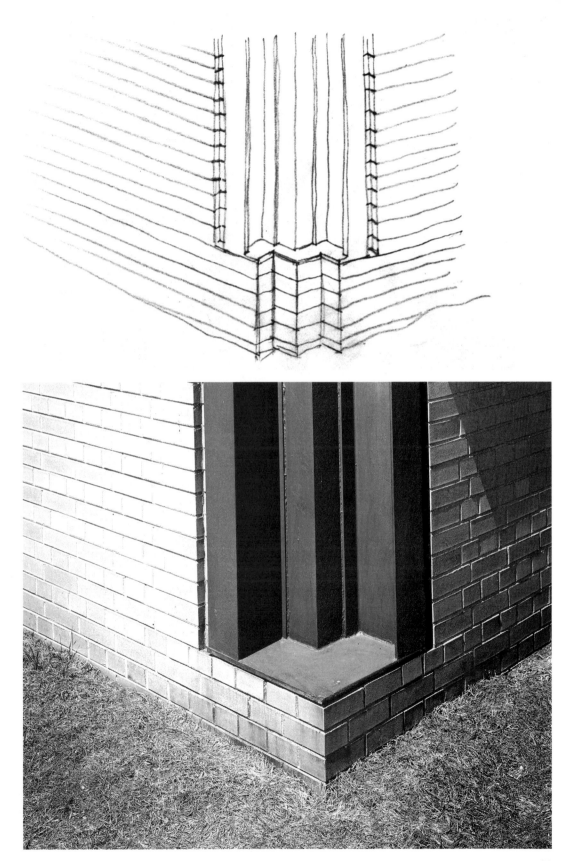

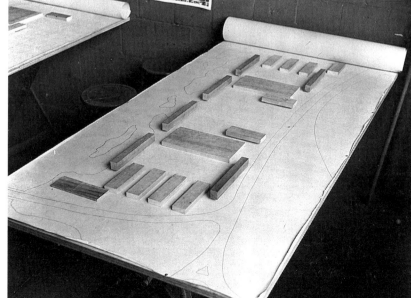

Illinois Institute of
Technology,
Chicago, 1942–57,
general view.

Layout design of the
campus, Illinois
Institute of
Technology,
Chicago, 1940–41,
model of a
suggestion.

Edith Farnsworth
house, Plano, Illinois,
1945–50, general
view and detail of the
glass envelope (photos
1990).

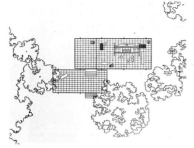

Edith Farnsworth house, Plano, Illinois, 1945–50, plan and view of the construction site.

The project was carried out without haste, the model of a first version being shown at MoMA in 1947. Building started in September 1949 and was completed in 1951. Mies himself executed wash drawings of the two versions, one sitting on the ground and the other raised above it. The latter version was eventually chosen. There are echoes of past projects here: the raised main structure returned to the design of the Concrete Country House and beyond to Schinkel's podium designs, while the glass walls recall the Tugendhat house and the Resor project. But the continuity stops here: the interpenetration of the internal and external spaces is not controlled or limited by walls, and the confluence of the forest glades takes place right in the interior of the glass volume. Nowhere before had Mies placed the structural columns outside the main volume; this accentuates the impression of levitation.[196]

While the eight I-shaped columns feature in the design from the outset, the box that they support has undergone some variations. At first the porch was enclosed, as the 1947 model shows. Then the position of the central core changed. At first tucked to one side, then placed markedly off centre, it moved towards the axis of symmetry, without ever reaching it. The building's corners are open; all the services run through the core and under the floor. It is a glass box, 28 by 77 feet (8.5 × 23.5 m), with its south face parallel to the river. There is a major transformation of the relation between the walls and the vertical supports: the unity of the IIT buildings is dispelled, and the columns seem more forceful than the horizontal elements; the whole house seems to have been hoisted into place. However, any sense of effort is belied by the tactile surfaces, the factory polish applied to the steel before painting and the finesse of the assembly of the floor slabs, which give the house a mechanical precision of finish. Moreover, its relative compactness is a long way from the tentacular outreach of the 1920s designs.

A fragile shelter perched on posts and traversed by the spectacle of the river and the woods, the Farnsworth house has nothing of the solidity of a masonry house. In the teeth of floods and storms, it offers, as Richard Sennett has remarked, a 'modern expression of the sublime'.[197] Indeed its lightness makes it more like a tea pavilion, a temporary shelter, than a permanent building imposing its ascendancy on its site. Mies perfectly expressed the modesty of this house in its relationship with nature:

[196] In connection with these columns Tegethoff mentions the precedent of the H.G. Chamberlain house of Walter Gropius and Marcel Breuer at Wayland, Massachusetts (1940): Wolf Tegethoff, *Mies van der Rohe; die Villen und Landhausprojekte*, op. cit., p. 131.

[197] Richard Sennett, *The Consciousness of the Eye*, New York, A. Knopf, 1991, p. 144.

Mies van der Rohe on the steps of the Edith Farnsworth house during its construction.

Nature should also live its own life, we should not destroy it with the colors of our houses and interiors. But we should try to bring nature, houses and human beings together in a higher unity. When you see nature through the glass walls of the Farnsworth House, it gets a deeper meaning than outside. More is asked from nature, because it becomes a part of a larger whole.[198]

The neutrality of the materials chosen – white enamelled steel and Roman travertine defining a beige plane which is intersected by the diaphragm of the entrance wall – is presented as an expression of just this deference towards nature, rather than – as has been suggested – the evocation of a sort of domestic temple, whether Shinto or Greek:

I think the Farnsworth house has never been properly understood. I myself have stayed in that house from morning to night. Until then I didn't know how colorful nature could be. We must take care to use neutral tones in interior spaces, because outside there are all sorts of colours. These colours change continually and totally, and I would like to say that it's quite simply magnificent.[199]

Mies's appreciation of nature was not reciprocated, however, and the building, which had no air-conditioning, had severe environmental problems: the windows were covered in condensation in the winter, and heat and insects became oppressive in summer, particularly as Mies would not allow any protection around the porch. In the same way the relationship between Mies and his client, which was cordial during construction, later deteriorated. Edith Farnsworth seemed, in Mies's own words, 'to have thought that the architect came with the house'. Although satisfied with the building, she took a fierce dislike to its author, and sued him for cost overruns in a legal action that was much reported in the press; Mies won in 1953. As part of a campaign against the 'Menace to the New America' represented by Modernist architects in general and Mies in particular, the Hearst magazine *House Beautiful* gave Farnsworth the last word.[200] Subsequently a collector's piece, the house, according to its present owner, Lord Palumbo, 'performs extremely well as a home for a single person'.[201]

[198] Mies van der Rohe, comments collected by Christian Norberg-Schulz, 'Talks with Mies van der Rohe', *L'Architecture d'aujourd'hui*, No. 79, September 1958, p. 100.

[199] Mies van der Rohe, interview for the BBC, May 1959, loc. cit.

[200] Elisabeth Gordon, 'The Threat to the Next America', *House Beautiful*, No. 95, April 1953, pp. 126–30 and 250–51.

[201] Peter Palumbo, 'Farnsworth Impressions', *Inland Architect*, March–April 1986, pp. 43–46.

Edith Farnsworth
house, Plano, Illinois,
1945–50, views from
the bank of Fox River
and opposite view
from the porch
(photos 1990).

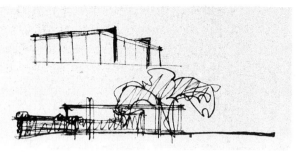
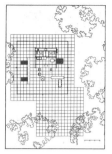

)ject for the Fifty By
ty House, 1950–52,
etch and plan.

Shortly afterwards, Mies designed a theoretical project for a house 50 feet (15.2 m) square – the Fifty By Fifty House. Again it is a simple box, but here the core is thicker. The roof, of a rigid, braced construction, is supported by four columns, one in the middle of each side, instead of eight. But the American dream of the post-war family house had little in common with this transparent box, which was to remain Mies's last major project for a detached residence.

At the end of his tenure at IIT Mies built Crown Hall, for the schools of architecture and urban planning, and the Institute of Design, a successor to the New Bauhaus, which had been absorbed by IIT in December 1949. Here he broke with the language which he had adopted for most of the other buildings, reformulating on a new scale the totally open configuration of the Farnsworth house and of the Fifty By Fifty House.

A single, uninterrupted space, 120 × 220 feet (36.6 × 67 m), with a height of 18 feet (5.5 m), Crown Hall is roofed by a spectacular structure designed by Frank J. Kornacker, which essentially consists of four large girders of welded steel, under which the ceiling is suspended. The main floor is completely open and suitable for any combination of tables and teaching spaces. The more technical facilities and the lecture rooms are relegated to the basement, reflecting an educative system centred on the workshop activity. The main entrance is approached by a steel stairway, covered in a skin of travertine, similar in its texture to that of the Farnsworth house. For Mies, this building was to remain 'the clearest structure we have done, the best to express our philosophy'.[202] But make no mistake: this reflects a new set of issues, not so much because of the size of the space – Mies aspired to these vast spaces, as if they represent an ideal habitation – but because the steel skeleton, which was exposed internally in the preceding buildings, is now invisible, as in the Farnsworth house.[203] Judged by Colin Rowe 'too pure to be useful',[204] Crown Hall is the first complete realization of Mies's idea of a big space where anything is possible, as propounded in the 1920s in opposition to Häring's strategies of adaptation to function:

> For heaven's sake, why don't you plan the building big enough so that you can walk freely and not in only one predetermined direction? We don't know at all if the

[202] 'Mies' Enormous Room', *The Architectural Forum*, vol. 105, August 1956, p. 105.

[203] See Frampton's remarks: Kenneth Frampton, *Mies van der Rohe: Avant-Garde and Continuity, Studies in Tectonic Culture*, 3, Houston, Rice University, 1985 (Craig Francis Culliman Lectures).

[204] Colin Rowe, 'Neo-Classicism and Modern Architecture II', in *The Mathematics of the Ideal Villa and Other Essays*, Cambridge (Mass.), MIT Press, 1976, p. 151.

Crown Hall, Illinois Institute of Technology, Chicago, 1950–56, view of the south west corner and general views (photos 1993).

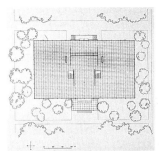

Crown Hall, Illinois Institute of Technology, Chicago, 1950–56, plan and view of the interior (photo 1990).

people will use it in the way we would like them to. First of all the functions are not clear and secondly they are not constant – they change much faster than the building. Our building lasts for several hundred years. What will wear out are the elevators, or heating systems, etc., but the structure will never wear out.[205]

In 1953 Mies used a similar structure of large girders, but in truss form, for his competition entry for a National Theatre in Mannheim, his first project for Germany since 1938.[206] In 1952, ten years after the Concert Hall, Mies and a group of IIT students designed a Convention Hall for the south side of Chicago, a covered space almost as big as the factory he used in his collage. The exhibition and congress hall, on a square plan with 720 feet (220 m) long sides, would have been able to accommodate 50 000 people. The two-dimensional steel truss framework was this time completely exposed, and supported by peripheral columns, freeing the whole covered area. This programme carried to its limits the theme of the great open space, and won Mies the congratulations of his former employer, Bruno Paul, who saluted this 'gigantic design'.[207] It was intended as part of an urban project carrying out the intentions of Daniel Burnham's plan of 1909. It was eventually built, in a somewhat different form, after Mies's death by his former assistant Gene Summers within the C.F. Murphy office.

Alongside these interpretations of the theme of the great covered space, Mies concerned himself with the elaboration and improvement of another architectural type that is characteristic of his American work: the skyscraper apartment block. These buildings were the first sign of a revival of building activity, which Chicago had been waiting for since the Crash of 1929, through two decades of urban stagnation scarcely ameliorated by the few buildings produced by Roosevelt's Public Works Administration.[208] The phase of growth that began in the city after 1945 ushered in a vast urban redevelopment programme. A massive influx of blacks from the South swelled the ghettos, while 'Boss' Richard Daley, elected for the first of his three terms as mayor in 1955, built up his political machine.[209] In 1946 Mies met the young developer Herbert Greenwald, who had initially intended to employ Gropius; it was Greenwald who enabled Mies to add to his IIT work a range of new residential buildings. In total Mies constructed six high-rise buildings for Greenwald, in addition to

[205] 'Mies in Berlin', LC, 62, p. 4.

[206] Hans Curjel, 'Die Mannheimer Theaterprojekte', Das Werk, vol. 40, 1953, pp. 312–15.

[207] Bruno Paul, letter to Mies van der Rohe, Düsseldorf, 20 January 1956, MoMA, personal documents, file 3.

[208] Carl W. Condit, Chicago 1930–1970: Building, Planning and Urban Technology, Chicago/London University of Chicago Press, 1974.

[209] On the ethnic form of the city during this phase, see: Arnold R. Hirsch, Making the Second Ghetto: Race and Housing in Chicago, 1940–1960, Cambridge/New York, Cambridge University Press, 1983. On municipal management of the city: Mike Royko, Boss: Richard J. Daley of Chicago, New York, Dutton, 1971.

the fourteen others that he built in Chicago between 1948 and
1969.[210]

The first of these were the Promontory Apartments on Southside,
near the Museum of Natural History, which Mies built for Greenwald between 1947 and 1949. The scarcity of steel in the immediate aftermath of the war led Mies to defer his preoccupation with
metal structures and build this block of 21 storeys with a skeleton
of reinforced concrete. Contrary to the impression given by all
the photos published at the time and since, the two sides of the
building are strongly differentiated. The façade overlooking the
lake is flat, the landward side has return wings that create a
double T-shape. A distinctive expression of the structure is the
sequential decreasing of the thickness of the external piers every
five storeys, marked by a horizontal setback and giving the façade
a kind of Gothic profile. Moreover the joints and recessed lines
which give the building texture when seen close up are not
obvious from a distance, because of the uniform beige-grey
colour of the concrete frame and the brick infills.

Even before the Promontory Apartments were finished, Greenwald (in partnership with Robert Hall McCormick father and son)
launched a second and more ambitious project, this time situated
on the Northside. The 26 storey blocks of 860–880 Lake Shore
Drive develop the original steel frame version of the Promontory
Apartments design. They are set at right angles, aligned with the
checkerboard urban pattern of Chicago, the irregular diagonal of
the shore defining a trapezoidal external space on plan. Through
their partially open ground floors, they form a filter between the
Near Northside and the lake front, motionless sentinels watching
over the expanse of water.

The main steel skeleton forms three bays on the end wall and
five on the main façade, each bay filled by four aluminium
window-panels; and this 5 × 3 proportion becomes a recurrent
feature in later projects by Mies. The initial purity of the structure
was threatened by the local building code, which insisted that the
bearing elements should be coated with 2 inches (5 centimetres)
of concrete. Mies obliged, and then encased the coated beams
and columns in a covering of steel to which non-load-bearing
rolled steel I-beams were welded, thus creating a secondary
framework joining the main uprights, stiffening the skin and

LAKE SHORE
DRIVE: THE
FIRST TOWER
BLOCKS

[210] John W. Stamper,
'Patronage and the City
Grid; the High-Rise
Architecture of Mies van
der Rohe in Chicago',
Inland Architect, vol. 30,
No. 2, March-April 1986,
pp. 34–41.

 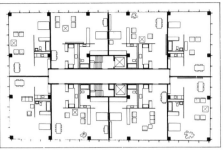

visually reinforcing the lines of force in a structure that is both hidden and revealed. Mies justified this transgression against the rationalist principles that he had always claimed to observe:

> It was very important to preserve and extend the rhythm which the mullions set up on the rest of the building. We looked at it on the model without the steel section [I-beams] attached to the corner column and *it did not look right*. Now the other reason is that this steel section was needed to stiffen the plate which covers the corner column so this plate would not ripple, and also we needed it for strength when the sections were hoisted into place. Now, of course, that's a very *good* reason – but the other reason is the real reason.[211]

The steel skeleton supports a secondary structure, into which the panels of the façade are inserted. The panels incorporate a thicker low rib and a recessed bar. Inside the apartments, the open plan which was initially proposed was replaced by partitioned rooms, and in the finished blocks silvery curtains keep out the sun and discreetly hide the choices of the tenants. The grey natural aluminium window frames chime with the glossy, dark linoleum floor and the white walls, in a harmony that frames the shifting spectacle of the lake. These buildings constitute a collective form, as oblique views confirm: when the glass panels disappear into the relief of the façades, an overall form appears, and this is now scarcely modulated except by variations in detail. In this context, Mies explicitly challenged Sullivan's dictum that 'Form follows Function':

> We do the opposite. We reverse this, and make a practical and satisfying shape, and then fit the functions to it. Today this is the only practical way to build, because the functions of most buildings are continuously changing, but economically the structure cannot change.[212]

The pleasure Mies felt on the building site recalls words he published in 1922 in *Frühlicht*, where he affirmed that it is only when they are under construction that skyscrapers 'reveal the constructive thoughts, and then the impression of the high-reaching steel skeletons is overpowering'.[213] He himself bought two small apartments in the complex, but took care not to live

211 Mies van der Rohe, quoted in 'Mies van der Rohe', *Architectural Forum*, vol. 97, November 1952, p. 99.

212 Mies van der Rohe, quoted in 'Mies van der Rohe', *Architectural Forum*, op. cit., p. 94.

213 Mies van der Rohe, 'Hochhäuser', loc. cit., p. 94.

Mies van der Rohe at
the window of an
apartment at 860–880
Lake Shore Drive,
Chicago, between
1951 and 1953.

Opposite page: 860–880 Lake Shore Drive, Chicago, 1948–51, view of the site during mounting of the windows.

Below: 860–880 Lake Shore Drive, Chicago, 1948–51, general view.

there, fearing, on his own admission, that he might be constantly confronted by the complaints of the tenants. He remained in a more traditional Neo-Renaissance residence with his collection of paintings (including a Picasso) and etchings. When a visitor asked why he had not built a house for himself – although he had designed one – Mies said that he would never have been able to hang his Klees and his Schwitters on the glass walls of his own architecture.

Fully exploiting the advantages conferred both by Mies's great reputation and by the financial and technical practices that enabled them to sell the apartments at 10% below market price, Greenwald and his associates undertook numerous developments on an unusually ambitious scale. As a result, the structure of Mies's office inevitably changed, since Greenwald expected it to generate all the working drawings. It also became more profitable, even though Greenwald seems to have used every possible stratagem to delay the payment of Mies's fees.[214] Mies was hard-headed in all his financial relationships with clients, and when Erich Mendelsohn, towards the end of his life, was hoping for new commissions, Mies was able to give him the benefit of his experience in the management of contracts and remuneration.[215]

The apartments at 900–910 Lake Shore Drive (also known as 900 Esplanade) were built for Metropolitan Structures, the firm set up by Greenwald and Samuel Katzin. They differ from the two earlier tower blocks nearby in their height – they are two storeys higher – and in their structure. Here the steel skeleton is entirely replaced by concrete, and the role of the metal façade no longer the visible expression of a concealed steel frame; its steel struts and panels of aluminium – now a relatively inexpensive material – lend an illusion of metal solidity to a hidden mineral structure, thus undermining one of the basic principles of Miesian theory. The lobbies of the two towers are fronted by a glass wall set back from the plane of the façades, so that the buildings seem to float above a volume of air. Only a fine horizontal black line betrays the presence of the concrete floor slabs.

During the same period Mies built for Greenwald, on exactly the same structural principles, the two high-rise blocks of the Commonwealth Promenade Apartments (there were originally to have been four). This time the marked contrast between the main

214 Joseph Fujikawa, in William S. Shell, *Impressions of Mies: an Interview on Mies van der Rohe; his Early Chicago Years 1938–1948*, op. cit., pp. 15–16, 24.

215 See the correspondence exchanged between the two architects in 1953, LC, box 40.

860–880 Lake Shore Drive, Chicago, 1948–51, an entrance (photo 1990).

900–910 Lake Shore Drive, Chicago, 1953–56, part of the façade (photo 1990).

columns and the mullions of the windows was softened, as if Mies was prepared to admit the fact that the whole of the exterior was simply a skin. These blocks transform the character of Lake Shore Drive, with their aluminium envelope in contrast to the obscurity of older blocks. Acting as a visual punctuation at the end of Lincoln Park, they stand out from the urban fabric of north Chicago. The space between them and a street intersection is occupied by a small swimming pool. The interplay of the large panels of turquoise glass and the aluminium offers a visual echo of the dominant colours of the lake, flooding the ground-level circulation area with colour.

The last project designed for Greenwald was Lafayette Park (1955–63), a modern development applying the notion of *urbs in horto* – the Garden City – formulated by Ludwig Hilberseimer. Situated 2.5 km (1.6 miles) from the centre of Detroit, the whole of Lafayette Park is one of the most successful of Mies's large-scale projects – partly no doubt because of its relatively luxurious finish and site management. The quality of the generously planted external spaces that separate the 21 storey blocks, and the quality of the housing itself, in particular the row houses and courtyard apartments, are a rare example of a successful collective development for middle class residents concerned to enjoy a suburban quality of life within easy reach of the city centre.[216]

When Greenwald died in an air crash in 1959, Mies declared that 'he was a man of our age'.[217] Two years earlier, thanking him for a present – a ceramic bowl – Mies had confided in him how much he wished that one day the buildings they had constructed together would be seen to be 'as American as this object'.[218] Bernard Weissbourd took over management of Metropolitan Structures, a company largely financed by the insurance corporation Metropolitan Life, which later extended its activity to other cities in the Northeast. Mies was forced to cut his office staff by half.[219] However from 1961 onwards he built the apartment block at 2400 Lakeview, on the edge of Lincoln Park in Chicago; it has a ground floor lobby with green marble walls. On a square plan, this building with its subtle outline marked the inauguration of Weissbourd's new policy of developing the smaller building lots in the north of Chicago. For his part, after 1960 Mies progressively lost interest in high-rise residential buildings, which he delegated

[216] See: 'Siedlung Lafayette Park in Detroit', *Bauen und Wohnen* vol. 15, No. 11, 1960, pp. 392–99; Lise Newman, 'Lafayette Park Detroit, Michigan; Mies van der Rohe and Ludwig Hilberseimer', *Modernist Visions and the Contemporary American City, Center*, 5, 1989, pp. 124–27.

[217] Mies van der Rohe, speech made at the funeral of Herbert S. Greenwald, 12 February 1959, LC, box 61.

[218] Mies van der Rohe, letter to Herbert S. Greenwald, 2 January 1957, LC, box 30.

[219] Joseph Fujikawa would follow the main part of these plans for Mies's practice.

900–910 Lake Shore
Drive, Chicago,
1953–56, entrance
halls (photos 1993).

Opposite page:
Lafayette Park,
Detroit, public
building and row
houses.

106

Commonwealth
Promenade,
Chicago, 1953–56,
general view and
view of an entrance
(photos 1993).

2400 Lakeview,
Chicago, 1962–63,
view of the corner
(photo 1992).

Opposite page: 2400
Lakeview, Chicago,
1962–63, façade over
the lake (photo 1992).

220 Joseph Fujikawa, in
William S. Shell,
*Impressions of Mies; an
Interview on Mies van der
Rohe; his Early Chicago
Years 1938–1948*, op. cit.,
p. 20.

to the members of his office.[220] From then on he concentrated on developing the finished form of the metal-clad tower, as he had devised it for these residential projects, into the big office blocks of which the Seagram Building was the prototype.

110

A classicism for the industrial order (1956–69)

Opposite page:
Seagram Building,
Park Avenue, New
York, 1954–58,
general view.

In 1954, when he received the commission to design an office building in New York for the Canadian multinational Joseph E. Seagram Corporation, Mies van der Rohe was 68. More than a quarter of a century after the first sketches of a Glass Skyscraper for Friedrichstrasse, here at last was his chance to translate his idea of a large office building into reality.[221] The president of the Corporation, Samuel Bronfman,[222] had originally commissioned a design from Charles Luckman's firm. This was rejected, and Bronfman's daughter Phyllis Lambert approached (among others) Philip Johnson, who was now director of architecture and design at The Museum of Modern Art. Johnson steered her towards a group of distinguished Modernist architects, from which, after an investigation lasting two months, she finally selected Mies. Mrs Lambert thereafter remained in constant touch with Mies in her capacity as Director of Planning for the Seagram Building.[223] Grateful to Johnson for publicizing his work through The Museum of Modern Art, Mies engaged him as his associate on the project.[224]

As a piece of urban planning, Mies's design was radically new. Set on a granite platform on Park Avenue, the Seagram Building, completed in 1958, dominates its surroundings, commanding a particularly solemn approach sequence which is flanked by a symmetrical pair of pools. The site occupies three quarters of the block between 52nd and 53rd Streets, with its frontage on Park Avenue, a former residential thoroughfare that was beginning to fill with offices. Instead of making the building rise straight from Park Avenue Mies situated his tower, with its ground plan based on his favourite 3×5 proportion, in the dead centre of the lot. This cost the client a considerable financial sacrifice, as he had to buy additional land; but Mies made symbolic amends by turning the Seagram Building into a major landmark, in both vertical and horizontal terms, on the landscape of Park Avenue. (Opposite stands Gordon Bunshaft's 1952 Lever House.)

The curtain wall stops above the ground floor, whose ceiling extends to form an entrance canopy, so the 38 storey building appears to hover over the ground. Mies stressed that for him this was not only a response to a particular problem but the definition of a general solution:

THE STELE OF THE SEAGRAM BUILDING

[221] Kurt W. Forster, 'The Seagram Building Reconsidered', *Skyline*, February 1982, pp. 28–29.

[222] Samuel Bronfman (1891–1971) founded one of the largest North American multinationals.

[223] Phyllis Bronfman Lambert, 'How a Building Gets Built', *Vassar Alumnae Magazine*, vol. 44, February 1959, p. 14.

[224] Johnson mentions – perceptively – the hypothesis of 'returning a favour' which obtained the commission: Philip Johnson, interview with the author, New York, 10 April 1991.

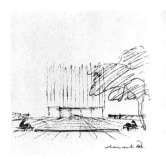

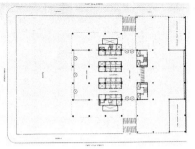

Opposite page:
Seagram Building,
Park Avenue, New
York, 1954–58, view
of the model.

This page: Seagram
Building, Park
Avenue, New York,
1954–58, sketch of the
plaza and ground
floor plan.

My concept and approach on the Seagram Building was no different from that of any other building that I might build. My idea, or better 'direction', in which I go is toward a clear structure and construction – this applies not to any one problem but to all architectural problems which I approach. I am, in fact, completely opposed to the idea that a specific building should have an individual character. Rather, a universal character which has been determined by the total problem which architecture must strive to solve.

On the Seagram Building, since it was to be built in New York and since it was to be the first major office building which I was to build, I asked for two types of advice for the development of the plans. One, the best real estate advice as to the types of desirable rentable space and, two, professional advice regarding the New York City Building Code. With my direction established and with these advisers, it was then only a matter of hard work.[225]

The mass of the building gives an impression of geometric unity, but the truth is more complex: it consists of two conjoined T-shaped configurations. On the four bottom floors, the main tower backs on to a rear block that occupies the full width of the site. On top of this block is a narrow central block of six floors, forming an inverted T. As at Promontory Apartments, the main tower conceals a central return wing at the back a single bay deep. The varying internal plans are unified by the fixed position of the vertical circulation shafts.[226] On the ground floor, the plaza leads without a change of level straight into the lobby, which is lined with travertine. Between the main tower and the rear block is a transverse galley parallel to Park Avenue, sheltered by two glass roofs designed by Philip Johnson, who also designed the restaurant, The Four Seasons, whose entrance terminates the axis of symmetry at the rear of the whole composition. The restaurant was built between 1957 and 1958 after various proposals for a museum or shop had been rejected.[227] Of necessity, the topmost floors of the tower house the mechanical equipment and are therefore opaque. The distinction between the base and the main block of the tower is strongly accentuated by the explicit presence of columns in the foyer, and the fact that above the foyer

[225] Mies van der Rohe, in Peter Carter, 'Mies van der Rohe, An Appreciation on the Occasion, this month, of his 75th Birthday', op. cit., p. 115. See also the remarks of Mies in his interview at the Architectural League, New York, n.d. LC, boxes 4–7.

[226] See Jordy's analyses: William H. Jordy *American Buildings and their Architects*, op. cit., pp. 251–77. 'Seagram Building, New York, USA', *Architectural Design*, vol. 29, February 1959, pp. 72–77. See also: Hubert Damisch, *Modern' Signe*, op. cit., p. 40.

[227] Notice for the registration of the restaurant *The Four Seasons*, New York, Landmarks Preservation Commission, 1989.

Seagram Building, Park Avenue, New York, 1954–58, view of a corner and detail of the façade (photos 1987).

they are invisible except at the corners, whose treatment is very different from that in the residential apartment blocks in Chicago.

The frame of H-shaped mullions in bronze, a material which is both matt and ostentatious – its use was criticized by Reyner Banham[228] – stops flush with the corner columns, which are themselves sheathed in a layer of concrete and a skin of metal. The horizontals present in 860–880 Lake Shore Drive have disappeared. Belying any pretence of structural 'honesty', the same façade formula continues on the upper service level, with its concrete infill.[229] The bronze colour of the whole building, which it would have been difficult to produce in glass, seems to have come from an inspiration of Samuel Bronfman who was taken with the colour of the old window frames of New York. The building thus offers the city a sombre reflection of itself, subdivided by the uprights of the curtain wall. Inside, the air-conditioning is set back from the façade and so allows the floor depth as it appears on the elevation to be reduced to a minimum. A strict regulation of the Venetian blinds, which may only be left in a limited number of positions, lends a visual order to the façade at all times. The measure of the building's success is conveyed by the warmth with which Lewis Mumford, a champion of continuity and organic use of space, hailed the contrast which it created with the meanness of the New York buildings in general:

> Out of this stalled, rush-hour clutter of new structures, brightly sordid, meretriciously up-to-date, the Seagram building has emerged as a Rolls-Royce accompanied by a motorcycle escort that gives it space and speed. To an even greater degree than its elegant neighbor, Lever House, 375 has *ambiance*. From three sides, it is wholly visible to the eye and approachable by foot; instead of using up space, it creates space. This act of detachment from the surrounding building was the most daring of all the innovations its chief architectural designer, Mies van der Rohe, made; by a heavy sacrifice of profitable floor area, he achieved for this single structure an effect that usually is created only when a group of buildings are placed together on a plot even larger than a city block, as in Rockefeller Center.[230]

[228] He considered it a kind of gimmick light years away from the 'industrial vernacular' of the Chicago buildings: Reyner Banham, 'Mies van der Rohe on Trial: Almost Nothing is Too Much', *The Architectural Review*, vol. 132, No. 786, August 1962, pp. 125–28.

[229] Philip Johnson, in John W. Cook, Heinrich Klotz, *Conversations with Architects*, op. cit., 1973, p. 19.

[230] Lewis Mumford, 'The Lesson of the Master', *The New Yorker*, 13 September 1958, pp. 141–58.

Seagram Building, Park Avenue, New York, 1954–58, sketch for a sculpture intended for the plaza (signed drawing, The Mies van der Rohe Archive, The Museum of Modern Art, New York).

The public commissions received by Mies van der Rohe in Chicago from the end of the fifties onwards fundamentally transformed the image of the whole city, in which he explored the possibilities of the skyscraper theme first proposed in New York (although Seagram abandoned a proposal for a building in Chicago in 1959). Built in the Loop, on the site of several demolished buildings (including the Federal Building by Henry Ives Cobb, a classical construction dating from 1897), Mies's Federal Center (1959–73) constitutes his most powerful statement in the very centre of the city.[231] Contrary to the original idea proposed by the authorities, for a single building filling the whole of the available lot, the Federal Center brings together the elements of the language forged for the Park Avenue site. Built on two esplanades of different sizes, its three rectangular prisms constitute a sort of autonomous citadel within the dense mass of surrounding office development. The comparatively low building along South Dearborn Street – the 30 storey Courthouse – is reflected in the glass curtain wall of the 44 storey tower, reinforcing the limits of the whole. In cross-section the interior of the Courthouse belies the image of tranquil repetitiveness conveyed by its curtain wall, the densely packed floors being relieved by the larger spaces of the courtrooms.[232] As sombre as Daniel Burnham's Monadnock Building, which forms a backdrop to Mies's complex, and which represents the swan-song of load-bearing brick constructions, the Federal Center is lightened by the granite paving at ground level, which laps upwards to line the entrance lobbies. The solemnity of the Federal presence is relieved by the generosity of the urban space provided by the plaza, which runs along the sides of the buildings in open galleries created by recessing the glass walls of the ground floor.

On the other side of the Chicago River, the IBM Building of 1967, with its 58 storeys, is the highest building Mies ever built. With its chilly, metallic presence, barely warmed by the granite floor and travertine walls of the entrance lobby, it rebukes the fantasy of the building next door, Marina City, designed by Mies's former Berlin Bauhaus student Bertrand Goldberg. Facing the Chicago Tribune of Hood and Howells, Mies also built the first stage of a massive programme for roofing the Illinois Central railway tracks; this was One Illinois Center (1967–70), overlooking the river in the form of a balcony with ingeniously managed

THE SKYSCRAPER VARIATION

[231] This work was designed by a group called Chicago Federal Center Architects, comprising Mies, Schmidt, Garden and Erickson, C.F. Murphy Associates and A. Epstein & Sons.

[232] Carl Condit, *Chicago 1930–70: Building, Planning and Urban Technology*, op. cit., pp. 129–34.

Federal Center,
Chicago, 1959–64.
View of the plaza and
detail of the façade
(photos 1990).

Opposite page: IBM
Regional
Management,
Chicago, 1966–69,
general view (photo
1990).

IBM Regional Management, Chicago, 1966–69, view of the ground floor (photo 1990).

One Illinois Center, East Wacker Drive, Chicago, 1967–70, view of the corner (photo 1990).

Opposite page: Westmount Square, Montreal, 1965–69, general view (photo 1990).

accesses and transitions. But it was in Canada that he built two complexes which combine the theme of the tower with that of the horizontal service block.

The first of these was the Dominion Center, built in downtown Toronto between 1963 and 1969; this combines two office towers with a spectacular single-level banking hall which represents the above-ground portion of an otherwise subterranean area. Mies took particular care in designing the executive spaces at the top of the highest tower.[233] The Westmount Square development in Montreal is more complex and no less interesting. Built between 1965 and 1968, it occupies the whole of a small block to the west of the city centre, marking the point where denser building begins at the foot of a residential hill. Only three of the four towers which were planned were built: two of them are apartment blocks, overlooking a two-storey commercial wing that adjusts to the slope of the ground towards the south. Access to all these is via the large plinth, initially faced in travertine and later ill-advisedly refaced in granite. In Montreal, as in the other complexes in this series, the space between ground level and the ceiling of the entrance lobbies of the towers plays an essential role. Its components are the layer of stone for the floor, a layer of air, and the white soffit that illuminates and levitates the buildings. At the intersection of the towers and the urban space, the large stone paving slabs in all these complexes recall the tradition of stereotomy from which Mies came, especially in the work on the joints – smooth, attenuated or effaced, in order when necessary to reconstitute the quarry bed.[234]

One of the few European projects in this series, which includes a building designed for the Commerzbank in Frankfurt, was to be set in the City of London, and aroused lively controversy. Designed for the developer Peter Palumbo from 1967 onwards, the 20 storey tower proposed for Mansion House Square aroused passionate debate among partisans and adversaries of the grafting of a Miesian skyscraper on to a historic setting. The debate was not resolved until more than fifteen years after Mies's death, when the project was abandoned, and it launched the Prince of Wales on his crusade against modern architecture.[235] As a result, the corpus of Mies's great towers was never completed. These works are repetitive only at first sight. Massive steles resting on transparent ground floors, supported by cushions of air, they are similar – in the strictly geometrical sense of the term – and yet

[233] See Detlef Mertins (ed.), *The Presence of Mies*, Princeton, Princeton Architectural Press, 1994.

[234] France Vanlaethem, 'Le Westmount Square', *Architecture Québec*, No. 71, February 1993, pp. 16–17.

[235] On these revealing polemics see: 'Mansion House Square' file, *International Architect*, No. 3, 1984, pp. 19–38; 'Mansion House Square Debate', *The Architects' Journal*, vol. 37, 1984, Nos. 28, 34, 36, 37; Joseph Rykwert and Martin Filler 'A Posthumous Mies: Two Views', *Art in America*, vol. 74, No. 4, April 1986, pp. 152–56.

Westmount Square,
Montreal, 1965–69.

1 and 2. General
view.
3. View of an
entrance hall.
4 View of an access
to the commercial
centre.

1	2
3	4

Opposite page: top:
Administration school
and social services
building, University of
Chicago, Chicago,
1962–65.

Bottom left: Tower No. 1,
Ile des Soeurs, Montreal,
1965–67.

Bottom right: Esso
service station, Ile des
Soeurs, 1967–69, partial
view (photos 1991).

Brown Wing,
Museum of Fine Arts,
Houston, 1966–69
(photo 1986).

subtly different, serving as foils to their urban settings, providing the standard for modern cities and holding out a mirror to them. Unique in the wealth of contextual associations which they propose, they rarely disrupt the urbanity of urban life – unlike almost all their imitators.

From the late 1950s onwards Mies's office worked on a considerable number of residential and public buildings in Newark, in Baltimore and Montreal, where it built a luxury retreat for the bourgeoisie on the Ile des Soeurs, in the form of large slab blocks subtly placed above the banks of the St Lawrence. The Esso service station – touching in its simplicity and rationality – which Mies built on the same site, for which he designed an overall plan, recalls the scale of the designs for private houses of the preceding decades; all its technical systems are concealed inside a long metal roof.[236]

Alongside his offices and residential towers, Mies rang the changes on the second major building type in his post-war work: the horizontal box. The theme of Crown Hall was taken up in 1965 with the rectilinear solid of the School of Social Service Administration the University of of Chicago – the only commission this institution ever gave to Mies – where it lays aside its solemnity by descending from its plinth. More horizontal than its predecessors, it uses window forms that contrast with the buttresses of the neo-Gothic buildings of the University. Its façades reveal the arrangement of its internal levels: while the entrance lobby and library occupy a volume corresponding to the entire height of the building, two lateral staircases give access to less spacious upper storeys lit on the façade by windows occupying the upper two-thirds of the elevation, the lower third serving to light a semi-basement.

The two successive extensions to the Houston Museum can be classed in the same category. Concentric, they use a curved geometry, unusually for Mies, who normally took the view that steel profiles were produced by rolling-mills and were of necessity rectilinear.

236 Anne Cormier, 'L'Ile des Soeurs' and Jean-François Bédard, 'La Station-Service de l'Ile des Soeurs', *Architecture Québec*, No. 71, February 1993, pp. 18–19 and 20–21.

Nationalgalerie, Potsdamer Strasse, West Berlin, 1962–68, detail of a ball joint (photo 1990).

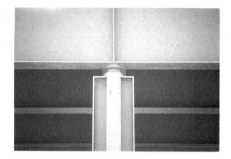

Opposite page: Nationalgalerie, Potsdamer Strasse, West Berlin 1962–68, view of the interior (photo 1993).

RETURN TO BERLIN: THE NEUE NATIONAL-GALERIE

During this period, Mies also pursued the development of a third major type: that of large spaces free from internal supports, of which the Fifty By Fifty House is basically a miniature version. The most important stage in this process was the design of an office building for Ron Bacardi in Santiago de Cuba, which was cut short by the Castro revolution. This project was influenced by climatic conditions: Mies abandoned the principle of the Crown Hall façade and recessed the glass wall under the shade of the overhanging roof. The structure of the Bacardi design – roof trusses carried by eight peripheral columns – was in reinforced concrete, but Mies then found the opportunity to transpose this principle into a steel construction, thanks to the project for a museum intended to hold the collection of the industrialist Georg Schaefer in Schweinfurt. It was from this design, prepared in 1960–61, that he evolved the Neue Nationalgalerie in Berlin, designed from 1962 onwards and built between 1965 and 1968.

The Berlin building allowed Mies to weave together in an obvious way the threads of his German and his American work. Elaborated by successive touches, the great steel omnifunctional exhibition hall sits on a stone platform, inside which the permanent collections of the Gallery are – it must be stressed – hidden away from natural light. Thus Mies returned not only to the theme of the pavilion, which began with the Riehl house, but also to that of the acropolis, as redefined in Schinkel's plan for Orianda.[237] Though to some extent it absorbs the slope of the land towards the Landwehrkanal, the platform's relation to the site is comparatively dubious – and basically just as unspecific as that of the second Glass Skyscraper.[238]

Having endeavoured for twenty years to emphasize the importance of rolled steel profiles, even to the extent of masking the real structure of his towers; having reduced the supports, in many of his European designs, to single vertical sections, Mies reverted with some serenity to the issue of the column.[239] In passing he took the opportunity of alluding to Behrens's *Turbinenhalle* by taking up once more the theme of the ball-and-socket joint – not this time connecting the columns to the floor, but to the roof. Such decisions could only provoke the scepticism of historians of modern architecture such as Julius Posener,[240] and the applause of those who, like Alison and Peter Smithson, had seen this 'reliquary' as a 'large box', accepting and making manifest the fact

[237] Fritz Neumeyer, *Mies van der Rohe, das Kunstlose Wort: Gedanken zur Baukunst*, op. cit., p. 49.

[238] Mak Jarzombek, 'Mies van der Rohe's New National Gallery and the Problem of Context', *Assemblage*, No. 2, February 1987, pp. 33–43.

[239] Didier Laroque, 'Le Secret', *L'Architecture d'aujourd'hui* No. 245, June 1986, pp. 5–11.

[240] Julius Posener, 'Absolute Architektur', *Neue Rundschau*, vol. 84 No. 1, 1973, pp. 79–95.

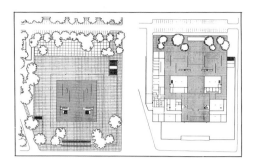

that art had identified itself with 'show business'.[241] This was nonetheless the expression of an extraordinary effort on Mies's part to restore logical unity to his reflections on the meaning of the great open space and of structural clarity.[242] After this majestic return to Germany, where his arthritis had forced him to entrust a large part of the on-site work to his grandson Dirk Lohan, he died on 17 August 1969.

Along with the multiple registers of his architectural work between the wars, the mature work of Mies van der Rohe is based on a rejection of invention as such and this relies on a limited vocabulary of types and themes, some of which overlap. Thus, the open floor of the skyscraper, with its vertical core, is akin to the designs of certain horizontal buildings, with their opaque central service area. Moreover, the visible structure of the skyscraper designs was transposed on to low-rise buildings, which borrowed their vertical elements, despite the engineering problems involved. This self-limitation was especially important because the work of improving the detailing and refining the ultimate designs absorbed a considerable part of Mies's energy. He used to cite the German proverb 'the Devil rests in the detail' (that is, the best of intentions can be thwarted by lack of care in carrying them out) and turn it on its head by saying that, on the contrary, God rests in the detail. Therein lies the key to this preoccupation. Hilberseimer said 'Mies spends too much time with an issue; he just can't decide'.[243] The mass of successive sketches of details of certain plans held at MoMA bears witness to his painstaking efforts.

In parallel with this meticulous work, not so much on the technical questions themselves as on their visual rationalization, another part of his energy was concentrated on the imposition of his typical grand forms on the landscape. Urban and sometimes suburban, this landscape was never a *tabula rasa*, but it was essentially a support for forms whose significance remained dissociable from their actual resting-place. Mies's bases, front steps and platforms define a negotiating space between essentially universal types and specific locations. The visual relationship of his buildings with these landscapes is moreover fundamentally different from that of Le Corbusier. Mies shared the latter's interest in framing, but replaced the notion of piercing with that of total openness, filtered by the perspective effects of successive partitions. Thus exposed to the exterior, from which they could

[241] Alison and Peter Smithson, 'Mies van der Rohe', *Architectural Design*, vol. 39 No. 7, July 1969, pp. 363–66.

[242] See, among the numerous interpretations of this building: Peter Serenyi, 'Mies' New National Gallery: an Essay in Architectural Content', *Harvard Architecture Review*, No. 1, spring 1980, pp. 181–89.

[243] Joseph Fujikawa, in William S. Shell, *Impressions of Mies: an Interieur on Mies van der Rohe; his Early Chicago Years 1938–1948*, op. cit., p. 33.

not be visually isolated except by items of furnishing – curtains and blinds – the interior spaces of his American designs eliminate corridors and tend to minimize the limitations imposed by utilities, or even to deny them outright – Mies's antipathy to plumbing was notorious. According to architects in his office, he was wont to say that the true grandeur of the Gothic cathedrals was linked to the fact that they had no plumbing.[244] In this sense, Mies stands at the antipodes of the New Brutalism, and in flat opposition to the ideas, for example, of Louis Kahn.

Totally aware of his place in the architecture of the twentieth century, Mies could not be accused of undue leniency in his verdicts on Le Corbusier or, especially, on Gropius.[245] His remarks on the latter always show a hint of a certain condescension; apropos of Le Corbusier, he liked to say how out of place the rough concrete of the *Unité d'habitation* in Marseille would have been on Park Avenue, where everyone was so well dressed.[246]

His veneration for Schinkel and Berlage aside, the architect he most respected was certainly Wright – and this feeling was reciprocated, as has been seen. But he never imitated Wright – or Le Corbusier – in their efforts to recruit clients. His painful relationship with politics – whether Left-wing, Nazi, or American – reveals both a certain lack of interest and, above all, a consistent refusal to compromise his work. Mies repeatedly and strenuously denied that he was a *Weltbesserer* (reformer), or that he ever wanted to change the world in ways other than by his architecture. In the 1950s he said that he had 'not wanted to change the world, but to express it',[247] and he repeated this to Dirk Lohan at the end of his life:

> I didn't intend to make the world a better place and I never said I did. I am an architect who is interested in construction (*Bauen*) and design (*Gestaltung*) in general, but one can also give a wider sense to construction.[248]

Over six decades rich in political, cultural and artistic change, Mies created a body of work distinguished by a constant effort to give rational form, intellectually and materially, to the designs of the elites that were committed to the transformation of society. Using steel and glass, the materials of heavy industry, in configurations shaped by the aesthetic strategies of the avant-garde but

[244] Joseph Fujikawa, in William S. Shell, *Impressions of Mies: an Interieur on Mies van der Rohe; his Early Chicago Years 1938–1948*, op. cit., p. 20.

[245] Regarding relations between Mies and Gropius, see Sigfried Giedion, *Walter Gropius, Work and Teamwork*, New York, Reinhold, 1954, pp. 17–18.

[246] Mies van der Rohe, interview with Peter Blake, op. cit., p. 98.

[247] Mies van der Rohe, interview with the Architectural League op. cit., p. 98.

[248] Mies van der Rohe, interview with Dirk Lohan, op. cit., p. 32.

nevertheless marked with the stamp of classicism, Mies produced categories of buildings as revealing of the world of capitalist production as the Florentine palaces were of the feudalism of the Quattrocento. In his early prototypes and in the variations upon them, Mies more than any other Modern architect reveals himself to be the exponent of *modernization* on the plane of form, definitively executing the programme which Peter Behrens had sketched out for AEG at the beginning of the century. His work thus reflects that other Chicago School, the school of the modern social sciences, founded on the 'crystal' that is the city with its populations and its ethnic and social groups, which provided an empirical basis for the creation of a model of conflict and arbitration that pretends to be universally applicable. Thanks to the possibilities opened up by IIT and Greenwald's commissions, Mies himself was able to design such models, but their reproduction by other architects, who did not bind themselves with the rigour of his control, proves that they were not reproducible. The mute presence of the bust of Mies by Marino Marini, sheltered in the safe ground floor of the IBM Building in Chicago, epitomizes his attitude towards the world. Carved out of the rock, his massive face looks out with sovereign assurance at his century, his mouth caught between a rueful scowl at the mediocrity of the townscape around him and an eager relish of the quality of the stones and the metal that protect him from it.

Biography

Ludwig Mies was born on 27 March 1886 at Aix-la-Chapelle, son of Michael Mies and Amalie Rohe.

1896–99: he attended the Domschule and, from 1899–1901, the Gewerbliche Tagesschule in Aix.

1901–5: he worked with various businessmen and architects in his town, then, in 1905, he completed a few months' military service in the Imperial army.

1905–7: he began as a designer with Bruno Paul in Berlin then, from 1908 to 1912, with Peter Behrens in Neubabelsberg.

1913: he set up his practice in Steglitz and on 10 April married Ada Bruhn, who would give him three daughters.

1915–18: he was posted in the army to Frankfurt, Berlin and then to Rumania.

1922: he joined the Novembergruppe, of which he became president the following year.

1923: he took part in the Exhibition of International Architecture organized by the Bauhaus in Weimar.

1923–25: he was a contributor to *G, Material für elementare Gestaltung.*

1924: he founded the Ring.

1925: he began a relationship with Lilly Reich, which would last until 1939.

1926: he became vice-president of the Deutscher Werkbund, for which he co-ordinated the Stuttgart exhibition in 1927.

1929: he was the architect for the whole of the German section of the International Exhibition in Barcelona.

August 1930–August 1932: he was director of the Bauhaus in Dessau.

1931: he co-ordinated the residential section of the Deutsche Bauausstellung of Berlin.

From October 1932 to its closure in July 1933: he was director of the Bauhaus in Berlin-Steglitz.

1932: Philip Johnson and Henry-Russell Hitchcock exhibited his work at The Museum of Modern Art in New York.

August 1937–April 1938: he visited the United States to work on a design for the Resor house and visited New York, Chicago and Taliesin.

July 1938: he was forced to resign from the Prussian Academy of the Arts.

August 1938: he emigrated to the United States.

October 1938: he became director of the school of architecture at the Armour Institute, Chicago, which became the Illinois Institute of Technology in 1940.

1940: he met Lora Marx, who would share his life until 1969.

1944: he became an American citizen.

1959: he retired from the IIT.

Ludwig Mies van der Rohe died on 17 August 1969 in Chicago.

Principal projects and buildings

List checked by information put together by Pierre Adler for The Mies van der Rohe Archive, The Museum of Modern Art, New York. Projects which were not built are in italics. As far as possible, the address of the buildings has been given.

Aloïs Riehl house, Bergstrasse, 3, Neubabelsberg (today Potsdam-Babelsberg), 1907.

Hugo Perls house, Hermannstrasse, 14–16, Berlin-Zehlendorf, 1911.

Competition project for a monument to Bismarck, Elisenhöhe, Bingen, 1910.

Project for the Anthony George Kröller and Hélène Müller house, Wassenaar, La Haye, 1912.

Ernst Werner house, Quermatenweg, 2–4, Berlin-Zehlendorf, 1912–13.

Project for a house for the architect, Werder, 1914.

Franz Urbig house, Luisenstrasse, 9, Neubabelsberg, 1917.

Maximilian Kempner house, Sophienstrasse, 5–7, Berlin-Charlottenbourg, 1921 (destroyed).

Competition project for a Glass Skyscraper, Friedrichstrasse, Berlin, 1921.

Project for the Petermann house, Neubabelsberg, 1921.

Cuno Feldmann house, Erdenerstrasse, 10–12, Berlin-Wilmersdorf, 1922.

Project for the Georg Eichstaedt house, Dreilindenstrasse, 22, Berlin-Wannsee, 1922.

Project for a Glass Skyscraper, Friedrichstrasse, Berlin, 1922.

Project for a Concrete Office Building, Berlin, 1922.

Project for a Concrete Country House, Berlin or Nauen, 1922.

Project for the Lessing house, Neubabelsberg, 1922.

Project for a Brick Country House, Neubabelsberg, 1923.

Mosler house, Kaiserstrasse, 28–29, Neubabelsberg, 1924.

Project for the Ernst Eliat house, Nedlitz, Potsdam, 1925.

Project for the Walter Dexel house, Iena, 1925.

Project for a traffic tower, Berlin, 1925.

Erich Wolf house, Teichhornstrasse, Guben, 1925-27 (destroyed).

Social Housing Development, Afrikanische Strasse, Berlin-Wedding, 1926–27.

Monument to Aloïs Riehl, Klein-Glienicke cemetery, plot 122, Neubabelsberg, 1926.

Monument to Karl Liebknecht and Rosa Luxemburg, Friedrichsfelde cemetery, Berlin, 1926 (destroyed).

Velvet and Silk Café, Fashion exhibition, Berlin, 1927 (with Lilly Reich).

'Glass room', Deutscher Werkbund exhibition, Weissenhofsiedlung, Stuttgart, 1927.

Site plans for the demonstration housing estate and residential building for the Deutscher Werkbund, Weissenhofsiedlung, Stuttgart, 1927.

Extension to the Fuchs house (formerly Perls house), Berlin-Zehlendorf, 1928.

Competition project for the redevelopment of the Alexanderplatz, Berlin, 1928.

Project for the David Saul Adam building, corner of the Friedrichstrasse and the Leipzigerstrasse, Berlin, 1928.

Building project for a bank and department store, Hindenburgplatz, Stuttgart, 1928.

Hermann Lange house, Wilhelmshofallee, 91, Krefeld, 1929.

Joseph Esters house, Wilhelmshofallee, 97, Krefeld, 1929.

German pavilion at the International Exhibition, Barcelona, 1929 (destroyed, rebuilt in 1986).

Building project for offices and a hotel, Friedrichstrasse, Berlin, 1929.

Project for Emil Nolde house, Am Erlenbusch, Berlin-Zehlendorf, 1929.

Exhibition stands for German industry, Barcelona, 1929 (with Lilly Reich).

Fritz and Grete Tugendhat house, Černopolní, 45, Brno, 1929–30.

Apartment for Philip Johnson, 424 East 52nd Street, New York, 1930.

Mini-canteen at the Bauhaus, Dessau, 1930 or 1931.

Competition project for a golf club, Krefeld, 1930.

Competition project for a monument to the dead inside Schinkel's Neue Wache, Berlin, 1930.

House for a Bachelor at the Berlin Building Exposition, Berlin, 1931.

Vereinigte Seidenwebereien AG factory, Krefeld, 1931–35.

Project for courtyard houses, 1931–38.

Karl Lemke house, Oberseestrasse, 56–57, Berlin-Weissensee, 1932.

Project for the Herbert Gericke house, Berlin-Wannsee, 1932.

Refitting of a factory for the Bauhaus, Berlin-Steglitz, 1932.

Competition project for the head office of the Reichsbank, Berlin, 1933.

Competition project for the German pavilion at the International Exhibition of 1935, Brussels, 1934.

Project for a house for the architect, Tyrol, Austria, 1934.

Project for a service station, 1934.

Mining industries stand, Deutsches Volk-Deutsche Arbeit exhibition, Berlin 1934.

Project for the Margaret Hubbe house, Magdeburg, 1935.

Project for the Ulrich Lange house, Krefeld, 1935.

Project for an office block for the Vereinigte Seidenwebereien AG, Krefeld, 1937.

Project for the Stanley Resor house, Jackson Hole, Wyoming, 1937–38.

Preliminary designs for the campus layout, Illinois Institute of Technology, Chicago, 1939.

Design for the layout of the campus, Illinois Institute of Technology, Chicago, 1940–41.

Project for a Museum for a Small City, 1942.

Project for a Concert Hall, 1942.

Metals and Minerals Research Building, Illinois Institute of Technology, Chicago, 1942–43 (associated architects, Holabird and Root).

Project for the Library and Administration Building, Illinois Institute of Technology, Chicago, 1944–45.

Mooringsport and Meredosia electric power stations, Louisiana, 1945.

Project for a gymnasium and swimming pool, Illinois Institute of Technology, Chicago, 1945.

Alumni Memorial Hall, Illinois Institute of Technology, Chicago, 1945–46 (associated architects, Holabird and Root).

Perlstein Hall, Centre for Metallurgic and Chemical Research, Illinois Institute of Technology, Chicago, 1945–46 (associated architects, Holabird and Root).

Wishnick Hall, Chemistry Building, Illinois Institute of Technology, Chicago, 1945–46 (associate architects, Friedman, Altschuler and Sincere).

Boiler Plant, Illinois Institute of Technology, Chicago, 1945–50.

Edith Farnsworth house, Fox River, Plano, llinois, 1945–50.

Project for drive-in Cantor restaurant, 38th Street, Indianapolis, 1945–50.

Project for Cantor house, Indianapolis, 1945–47.

Promontory Apartments residential block, 5530 South Shore Drive, Chicago, 1946–49 (associate architects, Pace Associates and Holsman, Holsman, Klekamp and Taylor).

Electricity Station, Illinois Institute of Technology, Chicago, 1947.

Project for a theatre, 1947.

Institute of Gas Technology, Illinois Institute of Technology, Chicago, 1947–55 (associate architects, Friedman, Altschuler and Sincere).

Project for a building for the Student Union, Illinois Institute of Technology, Chicago, 1948.

Plans for the Algonquin residential complex Apartments, Cornell Avenue, Chicago, 1948 (associate architects Pace Associates).

Residential complex, 860–880 Lake Shore Drive, Chicago, 1948–51 (associate architects Pace

Associates and Holsman, Holsman, Klekamp and Taylor).

Interiors for the Art Club of Chicago, 109 East Ontario, Chicago, 1948–51.

Mechanical Engineering Building for the American Association of Railroads, Illinois Institute of Technology, Chicago, 1948–53 (with associate architects Friedman, Altschuler and Sincere).

American Association of Railroads building, Illinois Institute of Technology, Chicago, 1948–56 (associate architects Friedman, Altschuler and Sincere).

Cantor commercial centre office block, Illinois and Ohio St., Indianapolis, 1949–50.

St. Saviour Chapel, Illinois Institute of Technology, Chicago, 1949–52.

Project for the Leon J. Caine house, Winnetka, Illinois, 1950.

Project for prefabricated row houses with steel framework, 1950–51.

Mechanical Engineering Building for the Research Institute, Illinois Institute of Technology, Chicago, 1950–52 (with associate architects, Friedman, Altschuler and Sincere).

Harry Berke office blocks, Michigan and Meridian streets, Indianapolis, 1950–52.

Project for the Fifty by Fifty House, 1950–52.

Crown Hall, Illinois Institute of Technology, Chicago, 1950–56 (associate architects, Pace Associates).

Fraternity House Pi Lambda Phi, Bloomington, Indiana, 1951–52.

Robert McCormick house, 299 Prospect Avenue, Elmhurst, Illinois, 1951–52.

Carman Hall, Bailey Hall and Cunningham Hall residential blocks, Illinois Institute of Technology, Chicago, 1951–55 (associate architects, Pace Associates).

Commons Building, Illinois Institute of Technology, Research Institute, Chicago, 1952–53 (associate architects, Friedman, Altschuler and Sincere).

Project for the National Theatre, Mannheim, 1952–53.

Project for a Convention Center, Cermak Road, Chicago, 1952–54.

Commonwealth Promenade residential complex, North Sheridan Road, Chicago, 1953–56.

Esplanade residential complex, 900–910 Lake Shore Drive, Chicago, 1953–56 (associate architects, Friedman, Altschuler and Sincere).

Cullinan Hall Museum of Fine Arts, Houston, 1954 (associate architects, Straub, Rather and Howze).

General plan for the Museum of Fine Arts, Houston, 1954.

Physics-Electronics Research Building, Illinois Institute of Technology, Chicago, 1954–55.

Joseph E. Seagram Building, 375 Park Avenue, New York 1954–58 (in cooperation with Philip Johnson, Kahn and Jacobs, associate architects).

Project for the Lubin residential hotel, New York, 1955.

General plan for the residential complex at Lafayette Park, Detroit, 1955–56.

American Association of Railroads laboratory, Illinois Institute of Technology, Chicago, 1955–57 (associate architects, Friedman, Altschuler and Sincere).

Metals Research Building, Illinois Institute of Technology, Chicago, 1956–58 (with associate architects Holabird and Root).

Project for a commercial building for the Pratt Institute, Brooklyn, New York, 1957.

Project for the Kayser office blocks, 845 North Michigan Avenue, Chicago, 1957.

Project for a residential complex, Battery Park, New York, 1957–58.

Project for the Quadrangle Apartments residential complex, Brooklyn, New York, 1957–59.

Project for the Bacardi office block, Santiago, Cuba, 1957–60.

Project for the Seagram office block, Michigan Avenue, Chicago, 1957–60.

Project for the American Consulate, Avenida Paulista, São Paulo, 1957–62.

Complex of individual houses, Lafayette park, Detroit, 1958.

Complex of individual and collective houses, Colonnade Park, Newark, 1958–60.

Bacardi office block, Del Cedro, Mexico, 1958–61 (associate architects, Saenz, Cancio, Martin, Guttierez).

Home Federal Savings and Loans Association, Des Moines, 1959–63 (associate architects, Smith, Vorhees and Jensen).

Federal Center, federal and post court, Chicago, 1959–64 (in collaboration with Schmidt, Garden & Erickson, C.F. Murphy Associates and A. Epstein and Son).

Town houses, Lafayette Park, Detroit, 1960.

Museum project for Georg Schäfer, Schweinfurt, 1960–61.

One Charles Center office complex, Baltimore, 1960–63.

Project for the Friedrich Krupp administrative building, Hügelpark, Essen, 1960–63.

Urban plan, Place de la Montagne, Montreal, 1961.

Residential block, 2400 Lakeview Avenue, Chicago, 1962–63 (associate architects, Greenberg and Finfer).

Highfield House apartment block, Baltimore, 1962–65.

Administration school and social services building, University of Chicago, Chicago, 1962–65.

Meredith Memorial Hall, Drake University, Des Moines, 1962–65.

Sciences Center, Duquesne University, Pittsburgh, 1962–68.

Nationalgalerie, Potsdamer Strasse, West Berlin, 1962–68.

Lafayette Towers, Lafayette Park, Detroit, 1963.

Toronto-Dominion Center, Toronto, 1963–69 (architects John B. Parkin Associates and Bregman and Hamann, consultant architect Mies van der Rohe).

Westmount Square, Montreal, 1965–69 (working architects Greespon, Freedlander, Plachta & Kryton).

Martin Luther King Jr. Library, G 10 and 11 Streets, Washington D.C., 1966.

Project for the K-4 school, Church Street South, New Haven, Connecticut, 1966.

Project for an apartment block, Foster City, San Mateo, California, 1966.

Brown Wing, Museum of Fine Arts, Houston, 1966–69.

IBM regional management offices, Chicago, 1966–69 (in association with C.F. Murphy Associates).

Project for an office block for Lloyds Bank, Mansion House Square, London, 1967 (in association with William Holford and Partners).

Project for an office block for the Commerzbank A.G., Frankfurt-am-Main, 1967–69.

Residential building No. 1, Ile des Soeurs, Montreal, 1967–69 (working architect, Philippe Bobrow).

Project for Radio King Studio, Seattle, Washington, 1967–69.

Esso service station, Ile des Soeurs, Montreal, 1967–69 (working architect Paul La Pointe).

Office blocks on the plots of Illinois Central, 111 East Wacker Drive, Chicago, 1967–70.

Residential buildings Nos. 2 and 3, Ile des Soeurs, Montreal, 1968–69 (working architect, Edgar Tornay).

Project for the Northwest Plaza, Chicago, 1968–69.

Project for Dominion Square, Montreal, 1968–69.

Acknowledgements

The author thanks all those who kindly helped and advised in the preparation of this book, in particular Ariela Katz, Petra Marguc and Hasan Dolan, who assisted with the documentary research in New York and Stuttgart, and Lord Palumbo, who allowed him access to the Farnsworth house. He also expresses his gratitude to François Chaslin, who read the manuscript, to Pierre Adler and Terence Riley, who facilitated his research in The Museum of Modern Art, to Phyllis Lambert, who corrected some mistakes, to Franz Schulze, who gave him access to important correspondence, and to the Getty Center for the History of Art and the Humanities, where in 1993 he benefited from the best possible conditions to finish writing the book. He dedicates this book to the memory of Richard Pommer, whose criticisms he would have so liked to hear.

Further reading

This list only includes monographical works, classified in chronological order. The notes in the book acknowledge other publications.

Philip Johnson, *Mies van der Rohe*, New York, The Museum of Modern Art, 1947 (reprinted 1953, 1978).

Ludwig Hilberseimer, *Mies van der Rohe*, Chicago, P. Theobald, 1956.

L'Oeuvre de Mies van der Rohe, l'Architecture d'aujourd'hui, No. 79, September 1958 (monographical issue with a small anthology of Mies's texts in French).

Peter Blake, *Mies van der Rohe, Architecture and Structure*, Harmondsworth, Penguin Books, 1960.

Werner Blaser, *Mies van der Rohe*, Zurich, Verlag für Architektur, 1965 (revised edition 1972).

Werner Blaser, *Mies van der Rohe: die Kunst der Struktur; l'art de la structure*, Zurich, Verlag für Architektur, 1965.

Peter Carter, *Mies van der Rohe at Work*, New York, Praeger, 1974.

Ludwig Glaeser, *Ludwig Mies van der Rohe; Furniture and Furniture Drawings from the Design Collection and the Mies van der Rohe Archive*, New York, The Museum of Modern Art, 1977.

Werner Blaser, *Mies van der Rohe, Continuing the Chicago School of Architecture*, Boston, Birkhäuser Verlag, 1981.

Wolf Tegethoff, *Mies van der Rohe; die Villen und Landhausprojekte*, Krefeld/Essen, Verlag Richard Bacht GmbH, 1981; in English: *Mies van der Rohe; the Villas and Country Houses*, New York, The Museum of Modern Art, Cambridge, MIT Press, 1985.

Werner Blaser, *Il design di Mies van der Rohe*, Milan, Electa, 1982.

Franz Schulze, *Mies van der Rohe: Interior Spaces*, Chicago, Arts Club of Chicago, 1982.

Franz Schulze, *Mies van der Rohe: a Critical Biography*, Chicago, The University of Chicago Press, 1985 (published in association with The Mies van der Rohe Archive in The Museum of Modern Art).

David Spaeth, *Mies van der Rohe*, New York, Rizzoli, 1985 (preface by Kenneth Frampton).

Rolf Achilles, Kevin Harrington and Charlotte Myrhum (eds), *Mies van der Rohe: Architect as Educator*, Chicago, The University of Chicago Press, 1986.

Werner Blaser, *Mies van der Rohe: Less is More*, Zurich, Waser, 1986.

Arthur Drexler (ed.), *The Mies van der Rohe Archive*, New York, Garland, 1986–93 (14 volumes, introduction and notes by Franz Schulze).

Mies van der Rohe, European Works, London, Academy Editions, New York, St. Martin's Press, 1986.

Fritz Neumeyer, *Mies van der Rohe, das Kunstlose Wort: Gedanken zur Baukunst*, Berlin, Siedler Verlag, 1986; in English: *The Artless Word, Mies van der Rohe on the Building Art*, Cambridge (Mass.), London, MIT Press, 1991.

John Zukowsky (ed.), *Mies Reconsidered: His Career, Legacy and Disciples*, Chicago, Art Institute of Chicago, New York, Rizzoli, 1986.

Elaine S. Hochman, *Architects of Fortune: Mies van der Rohe and the Third Reich*, New York, Weidenfeld and Nicholson, 1989.

Arnold Schink, *Mies van der Rohe: Beiträge zur ästhetischen Entwicklung der Wohnarchitektur*, Stuttgart, Karl Krämer, 1990.

Franz Schulze (ed.), *Mies van der Rohe: Critical Essays*, New York, The Museum of Modern Art, Cambridge (Mass.), MIT Press, 1990.

Detlef Mertins (ed.), *The Presence of Mies*, Princeton, Princeton Architectural Press, 1994.

Picture credits

p. 50 *Hermann Lange House.* 1927–1930. Ground-floor plan. Pencil on tracing. 26¼″ × 37¾″ (64.4 × 95.6 cm). The Mies van der Rohe Archive, The Museum of Modern Art, New York. Gift of the architect.

p. 55 *German Pavilion, Barcelona.* 1928–29. Two plans. Sketch (possibly first idea for pavilion). Pencil on tracing, 8¼″ × 11¾″ (21 × 30 cm). The Mies van der Rohe Archive, The Museum of Modern Art, New York. Gift of the architect. Photograph © 1995 The Museum of Modern Art, New York.

p. 58 *Tugendhat House.* 1928–1930. Lower level. Ink, pencil on tracing. 19″ × 32¼″ (48.3 × 82 cm). The Mies van der Rohe Archive, The Museum of Modern Art, New York. Gift of the architect.

p. 58 *Tugendhat House.* 1928–30. Upper floor plan. Sketch. Pencil on paper, 8¼″ × 11¾″ (21 × 29.6 cm). The Mies van der Rohe Archive, The Museum of Modern Art, New York. Gift of the architect. Photograph © 1995 The Museum of Modern Art, New York.

p. 64 *Project for competition: remodelling of Alexanderplatz.* 1828. Berlin. Aerial view, photomontage (no longer extant). Photograph courtesy The Mies van der Rohe Archive, The Museum of Modern Art, New York.

p. 67, top *War Memorial.* 1930. Interior perspective. Sketch. Pencil on tracing, 8¼″ × 13″ (21 × 33 cm). The Mies van der Rohe Archive, The Museum of Modern Art, New York. Gift of the architect. Photograph © 1995 The Museum of Modern Art, New York.

p. 69 *Berlin Building Exposition: Mies House.* 1931. Exterior perspective sketch. Pencil on paper, 8¼″ × 11¾″ (20.9 × 29.6 cm). The Mies van der Rohe Archive, The Museum of Modern Art, New York. Gift of the architect. Photograph © 1995 The Museum of Modern Art, New York.

p. 71 *Gericke House.* 1932. Interior perspective of living room seen from master bedroom. Pencil on illustration board. 19½″ × 25½″ (49.5 × 64.8 cm). The Mies van der Rohe Archive, The Museum of Modern Art, New York. Gift of the architect. Photograph © 1995 The Museum of Modern Art, New York.

p. 71 *Verseidag Factory.* 1930–35. Interior stairs perspective. Pencil on tracing, 8¼″ × 11¾″ (21 × 29.7 cm). The Mies van der Rohe Archive, The Museum of Modern Art, New York. Gift of the architect. Photograph © 1995 The Museum of Modern Art, New York.

p. 72 *Brussels Pavilion.* 1934. Exterior perspective. Pencil on tracing, 10¼″ × 18¾″ (26 × 48 cm). The Mies van der Rohe Archive, The Museum of Modern Art, New York. Gift of the architect. Photograph © 1995 The Museum of Modern Art, New York.

p. 75 *Reichsbank.* 1933. Exterior perspective. Red pencil on tracing, 34½″ × 19¾″ (87.6 × 51.6 cm). The Mies van der Rohe Archive, The Museum of Modern Art, New York. Gift of the architect. Photograph © 1995 The Museum of Modern Art, New York.

p. 77 *Ulrich Lange House.* 1935. Plan with furniture placement. Elevation. Pencil on tracing, 13¼″ × 21¼″ (34 × 54.2 cm). The Mies van der Rohe Archive, The Museum of Modern Art, New York. Gift of the architect. Photograph © 1995 The Museum of Modern Art, New York.

p. 78 *Verseidag Administration Building.* 1937–38. Frontal perspective, looking northeast. Pencil on illustration board. 26⅝″ × 40⅛″ (72.7 × 109.9 cm). The Mies van der Rohe Archive, The Museum of Modern Art, New York. Gift of the architect. Photograph © 1995 The Museum of Modern Art, New York.

p. 79 *Resor House.* 1937–38. Jackson Hole, Wyoming. Unbuilt. Interior perspective of living room (view through north glass wall). Pencil, photograph on illustration board, 30″ × 40″ (76.2 × 101.6 cm). The Mies van der Rohe Archive, The Museum of Modern Art, New York. Gift of the architect. Photograph © 1995 The Museum of Modern Art, New York.

p. 80 *Illinois Institute of Technology Minerals and Metals Research Building.* 1942–43. Window detail. Perspective. Sketch. Pencil on tracing, 9″ × 11¾″ (22.8 × 29.7 cm). The Mies van der Rohe Archive, The Museum of Modern Art, New York. Gift of the architect. Photograph © 1995 The Museum of Modern Art, New York.

p. 85 *Concert Hall*. 1942. Unbuilt. Collage over photographs, 29½" × 62" (75 × 157.5 cm). The Mies van der Rohe Archive, The Museum of Modern Art, New York. Gift of the architect. Photograph © 1995 The Museum of Modern Art, New York.

p. 86 *Illinois Institute of Technology*. 1939–41. Aerial perspective. Early scheme. Pencil, charcoal on paper, 42" × 67¾" (106.7 × 172.1 cm). The Mies van der Rohe Archive, The Museum of Modern Art, New York. Gift of the architect. Photograph © 1995 The Museum of Modern Art, New York.

p. 89 *Illinois Institute of Technology Library and Administration Building*. 1944–45. Exterior perspective. Detail. Column base. Sketch. Pencil on vellum, 6" × 8½" (15.2 × 21.5 cm). The Mies van der Rohe Archive, The Museum of Modern Art, New York. Gift of the architect. Photograph © 1995 The Museum of Modern Art, New York.

p. 115 *Seagram Building*. 375 Park Avenue, New York, New York. 1954–58. Plaza sculpture. Sketch. Pencil on note paper, 6" × 8½" (15.2 × 21.5 cm). The Mies van der Rohe Archive, The Museum of Modern Art, New York. Gift of the architect. Photograph © 1995 The Museum of Modern Art, New York.

Index